Jean Giraudoux : Plays

JEAN GIRAUDOUX

PLAYS VOLUME I

★

JUDITH · TIGER AT THE GATES
DUEL OF ANGELS

translated by
CHRISTOPHER FRY
with an Introduction by
HAROLD CLURMAN

WITHDRAWN

New York
OXFORD UNIVERSITY PRESS
1963

Contents

Introduction

by

HAROLD CLURMAN

Jean Giraudoux, born in 1882 in the city of Bellac in the department of Haute Vienne in central (southerly) France, was the outstanding dramatist of that now "hallowed" epoch between the two wars.

He was a *Normalien* – a student of the École Normale Supérieure, that institution of higher education at which only the most brilliant students who aim at a professorship or the diplomatic service are given their final academic instruction.

Shortly after the First World War, in which he was wounded, Giraudoux, first a sergeant and then a second lieutenant, began his diplomatic career – a career he pursued for most of his life. During the early days of the Second World War, Giraudoux was appointed Commissioner of Information and Propaganda. Much of Giraudoux's work was written in the morning before he left to perform his governmental duties. A friend tells of visiting Giraudoux in the writer's office where instead of busying himself with official documents he was occupied composing a novel on French political life.

Giraudoux began writing plays in 1928 when he was forty-six. From 1909 to the time of the production of his first play he had written nine volumes consisting of novels, sketches and short stories and three other volumes of essays.

His iridescent style was often referred to as being the literary equivalent of impressionism in painting. Hailed by the majority of critics and derided by a few, Giraudoux's manner attracted more attention than the sparse narrative content of his novels. It was Louis Jouvet, the period's most celebrated actor-director, who urged Giraudoux to turn dramatist. His first play *Siegfried* was a signal success. He remained a dramatist for the rest of his days.

There are in all fifteen Giraudoux plays, two of which – *The Madwoman of Chaillot* and *Duel of Angels* – were produced posthumously – the first in 1945, the second in 1953. Giraudoux died on 31 January 1944 at the age of sixty-two. In Paris today a public school and a street bear his name.

With only one exception Giraudoux's plays have won unqualified success in Paris. For the most part they have been admired both in England and America and generally have proved "good box office". They are repeatedly performed and applauded in virtually every country of western Europe. Yet they are not "easy", not, in the ordinary sense of the word, popular plays. There has always been a certain ambiguity, if not indeed some resistance, in the public and critical reception of Giraudoux's work. It is interesting to inquire into the reasons for this.

Jean Anouilh once told the author of this introduction that it was his experience watching rehearsals of Giraudoux's plays (Anouilh had been secretary and man-of-all-work for Louis Jouvet) that gave him the clue to the direction his own writing for the theatre was to take. To the theatrical novice in the Paris of the late '20s, Giraudoux was a reminder that writing for the stage need not be a mechanical game of frivolous showmanship but a creative act, poetry. At this point of his "confession" Anouilh burst into an accurate and not unimpressive recitation of the most eloquent passages of *The Trojan War Will Not Take Place* (*Tiger at the Gates*). What Giraudoux had recalled to Anouilh was the true tradition of the theatre which had been abandoned and corrupted by the Boulevard Theatre.

When a Frenchman speaks of poetry in the theatre, his point of reference is not Shakespeare but the neo-classic theatre of Racine. Its vein is more formal and less romantic-realist than that of the great Elizabethans. The neo-classic French theatre is a theatre of art or, if you will, a theatre of exalted artifice in which life is fashioned, corrected and patterned after models of ancient and noble lineage.

To this tradition Giraudoux brought a touch of modern scepticism and irony, a trace of anguish often daubed with the smile of a salon seemliness. Giraudoux is serious none the less. There is steel within his froth, a wound in his gaiety. The charm of his mask is a form of the national *politesse*, the artistic prescription of the accredited French culture. It is one aspect of the stylization from which the French theatre rarely departs.

Whereas Giraudoux's forbears still believed in such absolutes as reason, honour, the State, sacrifice, Giraudoux's effort to believe is troubled. His plays dramatize debates in which traditional values barely triumph. The victories achieved are won at so high a cost that they may be accounted more damaging than defeat. A duality in Giraudoux may be discovered in every feature of his work: there is always some contradiction.

Most Giraudoux plays are comedies. (Giraudoux named *Judith* a "tragedy" – though its basic tone and final resolution is ironic.) Yet a certain element of bitterness marks a large part of his work. Much of *Tiger at the Gates* (which might be called a passionate comedy) sounds like banter but, as with *Duel of Angels*, it ends in disaster. Giraudoux struggles to remain affirmative, "optimistic", even lighthearted, but this is almost as much an attitude he requires of himself, a kind of self-imposed spiritual obligation, as a true faith.

The ideal of purity haunts Giraudoux's plays. He strives to cling to the absolutes which informed (and lent strength and stature to) the work of the traditional classicists. To do this he exaggerates his images of purity to the point of paradox and extravagance. Thus his "Lucretia" (Lucile in *Duel of Angels*) is a fanatic of feminine virtue – so much so that she strikes us for a while as almost laughable.

Ondine, in the play of that name, cannot live anywhere but in the freedom of the sea. She expires among men at court. The nobleman who loves her cannot make a life with her – her purity prevents it – yet he cannot live without her. In *Intermezzo* (sometimes called *The Enchanted*) the heroine – an almost faery spirit – is induced to compromise with commonplace reality and settle into becoming a cosy little housewife in a provincial town. But one feels that Giraudoux is reading himself a lesson in a mood of smiling regret. There is a recurrent motif of protest against modern *bourgeois* civilization in many of Giraudoux's plays, but Giraudoux knows no other way of eliminating its mediocrity, greed and conformism except by the fantasy of drowning the racketeers in the ooze of their own muck effected by *The Madwoman of Chaillot.*

Giraudoux is the persistent idealist in the last throes of his struggle to retain the dogma, the discipline and the hope of the past. What strikes Lucile down, the procuress says at the end of *Duel of Angels*, is "man's stupidity, and coarseness, and wickedness". For Lucile "swore when she was ten years old never to accept evil, swore to prove, even by death if it had to be, that the world was a noble place, and that human beings were pure in heart. Now this world has become empty and terrible to her, and life nothing but corruption . . ." Lucile does not wish her husband, who believes her guilty of infidelity, to know that she is innocent, for he, too, is corrupt through his suspicion. "He will live in a false legend," she says, "but what legends are true ? Truth is always the poor lamb being sacrificed . . . Heroes are men who glorify a life which they can't bear any longer." As she dies Lucile cries out, "The world has purity . . . beauty and light. Tell me so yourself." And Paola, her witty adversary, moved by the mystery of Lucile's suicide, replies, "It is true . . . for the moment." Thus Giraudoux in this his swan song.

Most of Giraudoux's plays are inspired by legends or myths – a typically French, and classic, trait – legends from other literary sources – German, Greek, Latin, Hebrew. What happens in those legends also occurs in Giraudoux's plays. But "what legends are true" ? The legends are seen in a new light, a light that distorts or diminishes them in a manner that is a compound of mockery and pathos.

A most striking example is to be found in *Tiger at the Gates.* Here everything is transformed by Giraudoux's irony and sorrow – which no amount of epigrammatic fun or Gallic scintillation can altogether mitigate. Hector – another idealist – is the general who having returned from war is determined to renounce it for ever. He contends with every agency that would bring about another war: the jingoist poetaster, the unscrupulous politician, the legal sophist, the uncouth captain, the sagacious statesman. Yet war breaks out – and all for nothing.

The play has appealed to many for its anti-war sentiments, but it has shocked others on the grounds that its "message" proclaims the inevitability of war. Giraudoux was proved empirically right – the play was first produced in 1935 – and he seems to have written it with his eye on the European situation of the time. Yet for this reader and interpreter of Giraudoux the play adumbrates a theme beyond the causes – psychologic, mystic, sociologic – for the outbreak of war. War is viewed in *Tiger* as the consequence of something inhuman and irrefragable in nature itself. It is a manifestation of Fate or Destiny – but not the Fate of the Greeks for whom it was the god above all gods and thus somehow "justified". Giraudoux's "Fate" is not evil: is a tiger "evil"? Evil is a human concept and nature takes no account of humanity.

It is characteristic of Giraudoux that nature's terrible force is given in *Tiger at the Gates* the doll-like, fetching shape of little Helen – a most original creation. She is sufficiently captivating to addle the brains of nations; yet she is wholly without sentiment, pity, morality or even thought. She is sensation – as close as a "living being" can come to resembling inorganic matter. She is gloriously indifferent. To seduce her is only a momentary and an illusory triumph. She will subsist despite all the exaltation and havoc she causes. Men will continue to wreck themselves to melt her and make her part of their human order. She turns the tragedy of the Trojan war into something akin to farce. But Giraudoux's play for all that (and perhaps because of her) remains poignant.

Homer and other poets of yore told their legendary tales. These myths, Giraudoux implies, did not tell the "real" story. Yet the myths remain: they have their own truth. But it is not our truth, man's truth. Hence the ambivalence of *Judith* – Giraudoux's most difficult play, in which the precarious balance that Giraudoux usually maintains with wonderful aplomb is constantly threatened. In this play almost all of Giraudoux's preoccupations, obsessions, and impulses are woven together to form a complex knot which does not unravel at first reading or seeing.

Here Giraudoux has split himself into two images: that of Judith the extreme idealist who is also a worldling, the pure young girl (Giraudoux's abiding symbol meant to represent the marvellous potential of a still unspoiled life), the virgin eagerly awaiting some pluperfect consummation; then there is the pagan Holofernes, proud of his consonance with the sensual world. He, too, is an "absolute" – of ecstatic pleasure in a universe without original sin. Perhaps the third figure which attempts to reconcile or include the first two, the soldier or guard who proves to be an angel, is even more truly Giraudoux himself.

The legend in the Apocrypha indicates that Judith slew Holofernes because he planned to become the scourge of her people, hence the enemy of God. This, says Giraudoux, may still be true. But his Judith kills Holofernes because, total romantic that she is, her one night of love with him is the highest point of her life, after which everything else must prove mediocre and shabby – like a middle-class marriage! Society, history, have no regard for such subjective motivations – they have their reasons which the human heart does not know – and Judith herself, imbued with a heroic sense of mission, is persuaded by the Giraldian imp – the angel of the last act – that she must yield to the wishes of the cunning rabbinate and tell the subjective lie that she killed Holofernes out of patriotism and religious fervour. Judith is thus the whore to whom the angel (in his mundane guise) blows an adoring kiss, and the saint that she finally consents to be. This is Judith's tragedy: that she accepts the role history or the law of man have designed for her despite the fact that the person she is is profoundly committed to the miracle of the flesh by which she was transfigured in Holofernes' arms. Perhaps, as a French critic has recently suggested, this situation is related to the form of Giraudoux's own life, divided as he was between his activities as poet and State functionary.

Because Giraudoux's theatre does not present characters so

much as ideational figures, it is necessarily a stylized theatre – anti-naturalistic to its very core. There are no "real people" in Giraudoux's plays. Their language is a written or studied language, deliberately artificial, uninhibited by the accusation of preciosity. One has the feeling in a first glance at the texts that hardly any one of the characters is expected to move. The plays are studded with *tirades*, long set speeches or declamations like operatic arias. One gathers the impression – as with Racine – of a certain aloofness (except that Giraudoux is frequently playful and teasing), even of coldness.

This has been called a "theatre of language". The French delight in language. Rhetoric, the parade and frolic of speech are tonic for them. That is why most French productions of Giraudoux display less movement than ours – and are more "statuesque".

This does not make Giraudoux's plays untheatrical or "literary" in the sense of being unsuited to the stage. They demand an elegant, often a sumptuous, picturesqueness, a subtle dance-like rhythm of motion to match the ebb and flow of the dramatist's dialogue. There is a kind of suave and Apollonian splendour in Giraudoux which modifies the ardour of his thought.

One recognizes immediately the difference between this and the English (or American) mode. The names of several of these plays have been changed in our theatre not simply to lend them a more sensational sound. *The Trojan War Will Not Take Place* is not even a joke to people vague about the *Iliad*. *Duel of Angels* was originally called *For Lucretia* ("Tribute to Lucretia" might be an alternate title), but who exactly was Lucretia? The French audience is not estranged by such titles as *Amphitryon* 38 (they know Molière's *Amphitryon*), *Electra*, *Siegfried* or *Caligula*, *Orpheus*, *Bacchus*. But they are all somewhat alien and forbidding titles in our play markets.

Tiger at the Gates was praised by the Press and well attended in its London production – it benefited by the presence of Michael Redgrave in its distinguished cast – and it was even more highly esteemed in New York. *Duel of Angels* – closer to the realism of modern plays of marital intrigue – was a greater success in London than in New York, though it played to packed houses during the national tour in the States, due in large measure to the public's interest in Vivien Leigh. *Judith* failed in London – as it had in its first (1931) production in Paris: apart from the play's intrinsic defects, it has everywhere presented virtually insuperable casting problems.

It is perhaps significant that all three plays were produced in London through American enthusiasm and financing. The brilliant and beautiful translations by Christopher Fry – the original texts have been cut, but are otherwise very slightly adapted – were urged and sponsored by three Americans: Robert Joseph, Roger Stevens, and the director of both *Tiger* and *Judith*.

This is not entirely due to chance. In *Dionysus in Paris*, a guide to the contemporary French theatre, the American critic Wallace Fowlie says, "The very refinement of Giraudoux's style will inevitably appear in certain periods of history a weakness, a lack of vitality." The English West End theatre was comparatively timid in the '30s and '40s, and after the breakthrough by Christopher Fry's own plays, the English theatre-going public began to hanker for (because it needed) a new naturalism, an abrasive and salutary confrontation of what once had been excluded from the West End playhouses – the particular life of the English working class. It would be a pity, however, if a new narrowness, the bigoted provinciality of the "revolutionary" novitiate were so to dominate the temper of the new audience that an earlier, more permanent – and even when foreign – broader tradition were to be lost. Giraudoux's dramatic work traces a wide path which marks the transition from the classic theatre to the mood which today has given rise to that new fetish: "the theatre of the absurd".

Judith

A TRAGEDY IN THREE ACTS

First performed at the Théâtre Pigalle on 4 November 1931 and produced by Louis Jouvet.

First presented in London by Roger L. Stevens, William Zeekendorf and H. M. Tennent Ltd at Her Majesty's Theatre on 20 June 1962 with the following cast:

JOSEPH	Derek Birch
FIRST SERVANT	Michael Culver
SECOND SERVANT	Alastair Speed
JOHN	Gary Watson
FIRST PROPHET	Alan Downer
JOACHIM	Michael Gough
PAUL	Peter Russell
JUDITH	Ruth Meyers
JACOB	Richard Dean
SUSANNAH	Vivien Merchant
OTTA	Tim Parkes
EGON	Peter Bayliss
SARA	Eileen Way
URI	Michael Culver
ASSUR	Simon Oates
YAMI	Roy Stewart
HOLOFERNES	Sean Connery
DARIA	Hira Talfrey
GUARD	Barry Foster
FIRST JEW	Andrew Kane
SECOND JEW	George Harland
FIRST JEWESS	Josephine Lindsay
SECOND JEWESS	Maria Lawton
FIRST CHANTER	Alan Downer
SECOND CHANTER	Simon Oates
THIRD JEWESS	Hira Talfrey
SECOND PROPHET	James Keen
GUARDS	Andrew Kane, Simon Martin
JEWS	Michael Culver, Alastair Speed
SERVANTS	George Harland Simon Martin

Directed by HAROLD CLURMAN

G.–B

ACT ONE

An ante-room in Judith's house.
Before the curtain rises we hear a kind of rending cry, a high-pitched male voice, calling, "Judith! Judith!"
As the curtain rises Servants appear on every side with clubs and swords in their hands. Judith's uncle, Joseph, urges them on.

JOSEPH: On the stairs! In the cupboards! Up the chimneys! Search for him! He won't get away this time. I'll make it well worth any man's while to find him!

1ST SERVANT: We shan't find him.

JOSEPH: Look for him, my good fellow. He's somewhere here.

1ST SERVANT: He's here, and he's not here.

JOSEPH: What do you mean?

1ST SERVANT: His voice is here, we all know that. But his body isn't.

2ND SERVANT: It's the voice of a ghost. We've heard it everywhere ever since yesterday, in the house and out of it.

1ST SERVANT: It's the dead who are calling your niece. Everybody knows that. And there's nobody but Judith who can save us. Judith, Judith.

Without realizing it he has reproduced the intonation of the calling voice. The other Servants shudder.

JOSEPH: Stop that. Haven't any of you found anything?

2ND SERVANT: Nothing at all.

The Servants go out. Joseph looks round suspiciously and goes. Almost immediately the window is quietly opened. A man appears and sits astride the sill. He cups his hands to his mouth and in the same strident voice calls, "Judith! Judith! Save us!" Joseph and the Servants rush in again. But the window is already shut. There is an immediate violent knocking on the door.

JOSEPH: Who is there?

JOHN: It is I. John. Open the door, Joseph. I've caught him.

3

(*They open the door. John, a young officer, pushes the man into the room.*) He dropped down from the window, straight into my hands. We'd better teach him that some names are too good for his mouth. Who are you?

JOSEPH: He is filthy and smells. I should say he's a prophet.

1ST SERVANT: The town is full of them. A sick nation gets prophets like a dying dog gets fleas.

JOHN: Well, speak, will you? Tell us your name.

The Prophet raises himself as though to speak, and calls, "Judith! Judith!"

JOSEPH: They're all alike. When I came in tonight I had to pick my way over the beggars lying in the porch. They called out for Judith in their sleep. The scum of the city dream of her. . . . Gag him.

JOHN: Let's hear what he has to say. It might be useful.

PROPHET: The fairest and purest of our daughters . . .

JOSEPH: There it is; the same prophetic nonsense. The fairest and purest of our daughters has to present herself to Holofernes.

JOHN: Meaning Judith!

PROPHET: Judith! Save us!

JOSEPH: Gag him, and take him down to the cellars. (*The servants carry the Prophet away. Only the First Servant stays.*) Well, what do you want?

SERVANT: Let Judith do it, sir; let her save us.

Joseph threatens him and he runs off.

JOHN: I hope she's not here.

JOSEPH: She is still at the hospital, looking after the wounded. I am waiting for her.

JOHN: Have you warned her?

JOSEPH: Of what? What's on your mind?

JOHN: They're determined to make a sacrifice of her. The Council has decided. They intend to send Judith to Holofernes this evening. I am only a few minutes ahead of the High Priest. He is coming here himself to persuade her.

JOSEPH: He will find me.

JOHN: What can you do? The whole city supports him. Did you go out this afternoon?

JOSEPH: I did.

JOHN: And didn't you see the same confounded slogan, scrawled all over the town: "Let the fairest and purest of our daughters go to Holofernes"?

JOSEPH: I saw.

JOHN: The whole population, hysterical and starving, desperate for a miracle, shouting all the time for Judith.

JOSEPH: You can hear them now. (*Cries of "Judith" from the street.*) Her name is like opium to them. This extraordinary worship they have for her is just an excuse for interfering with another person's life. Their piety's a chance to meddle in God's affairs.

Cries of "Judith".

JOHN: Judith! Judith! The name which has always meant for us the flower, the ultimate secret, a silence held in the heart; and now listen how they hammer at it, bark it out, turn it into a harsh, sterile cry for the rest of time. There are thousands of them trailing after the High Priest. What can you do against them?

JOSEPH: If Judith means to receive them, she will receive them. She has plenty of common sense. She knows how to take care of herself.

JOHN: In our present condition, starving and on the verge of being massacred, only the wildest nonsense will seem like common sense. So in fact the priests are being logical. The common sense is theirs.

JOSEPH: Is that what you came to tell me?

JOHN: I came to try to save Judith. If the priests do manage to see her, make her promise not to decide anything until she has spoken to me. I'll come back before very long; I have my own plan. (*He opens the main door.*) They're suddenly very silent . . . The procession has arrived. What a sinister silence it is.

JOSEPH: Get away now.

John slips out through a side door as Paul and Joachim enter.

JOACHIM: Where is your niece?

JOSEPH: What do you want with her?

PAUL: Joachim is the High Priest. He can visit a young Jewess without giving his reason.

JOSEPH: Not if he means to make a great heroine of her, a woman forced out of her natural destiny.

JOACHIM: Blame the people who have leapt at the prophecy. They've lived on it, instead of bread, for three hungry days. And now it has to be accomplished.

JOSEPH: I am a banker. Don't talk to me about prophecies. Call it mass hysteria.

JOACHIM: And I'm to suppose that standing before me is the only clear-sighted Jew?

JOSEPH: If you're not a great hypocrite, yes.

JOACHIM: And with those eyes which nothing can throw dust into, I take it that you can see our city freed from siege and ruin, our trade restored, the people fed and fat?

JOSEPH: I see famine and pestilence all round me. The least breath of wind, from either north or south, tells me that between Holofernes and here we're encircled by an army of corpses. What I can't see, I'm afraid, is my people saving themselves by a savage, infamous act.

PAUL: What do you see, then, between the people today and the merciless massacre tomorrow, when your niece won't be faced with the chieftain but with the brutal conqueror? Do you see what a sacred population in the grip of calamity calls a miracle? Perhaps you do: you see the dead rising in the trenches at the cry of "Stand up, you dead", or angels leading our infantry with bright, impregnable swords; or the great enemy battered to the ground by an apoplexy of remorse. That, no doubt, is how bankers usually view a hopeless situation?

JOSEPH: If you like. We will wait for the miracle.

JOACHIM: No need to wait, Joseph: the miracle is here. After six months of martyrdom, this city, which was blind and deaf, can suddenly see and hear again, at the sound of your niece's name. The idea has come to it to make her its leader. Well and good. When the meshing gears seem to want to bite on themselves for ever, only the finger of a child or a girl can slip between them and stop the machine, the finger of a David, the finger of a Jael, the finger of Judith.

JOSEPH: Forget the finger of Judith.

JOACHIM: Is she here?

JOSEPH: Go from here, before she returns.

JOACHIM: The men and women in the street have chosen Judith, and the more I think of her the more I have the same faith. I have watched her very deeply over the years. She is beautiful and knows she is beautiful. She is rich, and she means to use every advantage and happiness that wealth can give her. Already at twenty years old she has her own circle of men-of-letters, her model farm, her hospital, her collections as fine as any in the world. She's a good horse-woman. She dances well. She loves to make a brilliant entrance into theatres and restaurants, or, as it has to be now, into that harmless male harem, the military hospital. At one time I was irritated by the fashionable modelling of her hair over such an intelligent head, by the confident beauty of her walk. Today, I'm glad of these things: for God can find in them a way of taking her into his hands.

JOSEPH: Forget the beauties of Judith.

JOACHIM: How does she herself feel about being chosen by the people?

JOSEPH: We have other things to talk about.

PAUL: Does she know about it?

JOSEPH: How could she help knowing? Our house is more closely besieged than the city itself. It's crammed with flowers and presents of every sort. Of course she knows!

JOACHIM: And is it altering her life a little: how she dresses, and what she eats? There is a trace of a scent in the room, which smells good in your house. The process of change from a human being into the figure of heroic legend is brought about always in ways hardly to be noticed; in little presents given to friends, by way of the pressure of the hand on those who are close to the heart. Does this happen in this already sacred place?

JOSEPH: Sacred? Why sacred? I very much hope this place will never be sacred! The reason this room is blessed is because it is human, not because it is holy.

JOACHIM: That is for Judith to decide, not you.

JOSEPH: She can decide tomorrow, if she likes. This evening she stays in safety.

Enter Judith and little Jacob.

JUDITH: Greeting, Joachim. Good evening, uncle. Have you any bread for little Jacob? I found him on the stairs. Look at him. He's dying of hunger.

JACOB: I don't want any bread.

JUDITH: What is it you want then, darling?

JACOB: I want the most beautiful and purest of our daughters to go to Holofernes' camp.

JUDITH: I see. You've learnt your lesson very well. And what will she do at Holofernes' camp?

JACOB: I don't know.

JUDITH: Will she cut off his head? Will she dance with him? What will she do?

JACOB: I don't know.

JUDITH: You're a dear little boy. But first of all won't you have some bread?

JACOB: No, I won't have any bread.

JUDITH: What about some meat, then: will you eat that?

JACOB: Some meat? Real meat?

JUDITH: Uncle, let him have some meat.

JOSEPH: Run away, then, and get it, boy!

Jacob runs off.

JUDITH: Don't be so angry. He was only repeating what he had been taught at school. There. I have to kiss you, and don't try to escape it. The High Priest won't mind a little family

affection . . . And now, if you will, leave me alone with
him.

JOSEPH: I beg of you, my little Judith, do beware of Joachim.

JOACHIM: It is God who is here, not Joachim.

JOSEPH: Beware of God, Judith. (*He leaves them.*)

JOACHIM: It is true, Judith; God is here.

JUDITH: Alas, Joachim, I think He has made a mistake in
coming to this house.

JOACHIM: In no way. The prophecy says the fairest and the
purest. It doesn't say the most modest and retiring.

JUDITH: Does it say the most frivolous, the most capricious,
the most changeable? I am all these things as well.

JOACHIM: If you know of someone more worthy, name her to
me.

JUDITH: Involve a friend in such a doubtful adventure as this?
That would be too cowardly. Any woman who was brave
enough, whatever her face and body might be, would be the
purest and most beautiful. That is what the prophecies have
tried to say.

JOACHIM: I am afraid not, Judith. The letter of the prophecy
is unmistakable. Our God isn't a Greek god. He doesn't
speak in riddles and enigmas. He calls each thing by its
name.

JUDITH: And yet strangely enough I still don't hear Judith
named.

JOACHIM: Do you hear Martha named, or Ruth, or Esther,
or any other of your friends?

JUDITH: Why not look for her on some less distinguished level?
Among the minor officials in the Civil Service, for instance.
There is less jealousy there, and a good deal more virginity.

JOACHIM: Judith!

JUDITH: Or among the workers. You're quite wrong if you
think that God chooses heroes and saints only from the
aristocracy. Our history is becoming too much like a reference book of the landed gentry. The son of a shipowner kills
Goliath, the nephew of a banker makes the sun stand still in
the sky. Be more democratic. Give the Levys a chance.

JOACHIM: Restrain your wit. All these rejected ones are precisely those who have chosen you.

JUDITH: The choice of the people God hasn't chosen can hardly be of much interest.

JOACHIM: I didn't expect to hear you resist the voice of God.

JUDITH: I tell you again, for me it isn't the voice of God. Do you think, ever since the city decided that I was ordained to save it, I haven't been trying to seize on any sign addressed by God to me? The barest hint would be enough.

JOACHIM: A burning bush? An aureole round your uncle's head?

JUDITH: A murmur, a word, a breath, anything. When I was a child I would hear it, telling me to look up to the sky and let the sharp rain beat on my face. In the falling sunlight, one shaft would suddenly shine with a particular metallic strangeness, where He was regarding me. But not now, nothing today, even though I leaned closer over the wounded men, thinking He might cause their wounds to speak to me for him. But I heard nothing except the plaint of the wounded. Two died in my arms, and all I held was death.

JOACHIM: Does that great silence, that overwhelming absence, say nothing to you?

Little Jacob appears in the doorway.

PAUL: What do you want now?

JACOB: I don't want the meat either.

JUDITH: Surely you're hungry, Jacob?

JACOB: And I don't want cheese, and I don't want cake.

JUDITH: An apple, wouldn't you like an apple? We have still one apple in the house.

JACOB: An apple.

PAUL: Keep your apple, Judith. You know very well they'll make him bring it back again.

JACOB: Perhaps an apple . . .

JUDITH: Take your apple and go! (*Exit Jacob.*) Thank you, Joachim, for not telling me that God is speaking to me out of the mouths of children.

JOACHIM: The mouths of children speak to you of childhood. And yet all our children have suffered hunger and fasting for the past two days. That should be enough to move you.

JUDITH: Children don't know what happens when a young girl and a giant are shut up alone in a narrow room.

JOACHIM: Do you know yourself?

JUDITH: A little. In a dream I have struggled all night long against Goliath.

JOACHIM: Who had the victory?

JUDITH: He did, in the night, in the dream. But in the morning, I did.

JOACHIM: A bad preparation, but a good omen. And what's more, if you're afraid of the struggle you strengthen your chance of victory.

JUDITH: I do beg you, look elsewhere. I am told there's a girl living in the Lower Road, who suffered a visitation several days ago. Stigmata appeared on her breast and tongue, and her name is also Judith. There surely is the real Judith.

JOACHIM: I have seen this Judith. She has the face of a pug.

JUDITH: There's a rumour that Holofernes is short of ammunition. They say he is having to melt down all his jewellery to make arrows.

JOACHIM: That, in fact, is the rumour. And we started it. But the reverse is the truth. We have no weapons left.

JUDITH: But those three thousand Syrians who were on their way?

JOACHIM: They arrived this morning. But to reinforce Holofernes, not us.

JUDITH: Then so much the better for our army. Its merit will be all the greater.

JOACHIM: Our army? Our army, Judith, has ceased to exist.

JUDITH: What are you telling me?

PAUL: The truth.

JUDITH: A priest's truth. The officers will tell a different story.

PAUL: Will you believe an officer, then? John, for example; will you believe him?

JUDITH: Why John?

JOACHIM: You are betrothed to him, isn't that so?

JUDITH: And if it is—

JOACHIM: If it is, leave John to us. If you are hesitating because of him, we shall be able to convince him . . .

JUDITH: Convince him of what?

JOACHIM: That he has to let you go, to let you go as a heroine, and receive you back as a saint.

JUDITH: A saint seduced?

JOACHIM: Judith, who are you to dare to talk to me like this?

JUDITH: I will tell you who I am. Or John will tell you. God has certainly sent him here, so that I can also question him. I am not betrothed to him. But when he has answered me, then you are going to doubt if I'm the one concerned in the prophecy.

At a gesture from Joachim, Paul admits John.

JOHN: Paul tells me you want to see me. What is it?

JOACHIM: There are two questions to ask you. Is it true that this morning all that was left of our guard mutinied, killed their officers, and went over to the enemy?

JUDITH: A lie.

JOACHIM: Is it a lie that at noon today our best battalion panicked and fled, deserting its flag in broad daylight? We can see it, can we not, dangling its humiliation from the walls?

JUDITH: It's false. I know that it's false—

JOACHIM: In short, is it correct that the only defence we have now is a troop of old customs officers barely enough in peacetime to stop housewives smuggling butter into the city? Answer me.

JUDITH: Well, answer him!

JOHN: You are cruel, Judith.

JUDITH: I have eyes to see, and the answer is clear in your face.

JOHN: Thank God.

JUDITH: Do you also thank Him for being defeated?

JOHN: Be careful. You are the first person in the city to say that word.

JUDITH: I'm not afraid of words. Your whole bearing and body are shouting it at me.

JOHN: Spare me, Judith.

JUDITH: So you're beaten! Our superb army is an army of defeated men. Our colonels, and captains, and handsome lieutenants are all beaten.

JOHN: So we are less handsome now, is that it?

JUDITH: Hideous, you're hideous! What difference is there between the look of defeat in a soldier's eyes and the look of cowardice?

JOHN: Don't exaggerate. I can still look you in the face.

JUDITH: If you could really see me you would lower your eyes. If you could see what I am at this moment, from head to foot: a country made a fool of, confidence betrayed; you wouldn't be able to bear my presence here, you would turn and run as fast as you ran from the enemy. Only a short time ago I saw you in the street. The children were running to meet you, and the women were cheering you. They ran cheering to welcome defeat; and how it seems to shine through all the defeated! The broken ramparts, the howling dogs, the bowed heads of old men and children, are all touched by the light. It's only the beaten soldier who is dark and terrible. Flags and trumpets and decorations have suddenly turned into the filth of the gutter.

JOHN: What do you ask? Don't come to me.

JUDITH: I have to touch you so that I know how cold defeated armour is. And kiss you, to have the taste of defeated flesh.

JOHN: You are young, Judith.

JUDITH: What shall I know, being older?

JOHN: You will know there is no such thing as victory or defeat, or shame or glory, for the true soldier: there is only the battle, which has two faces, the bright or the dark.

JUDITH: Are you fighting now?

JOHN: I was fighting until noon. I shall be fighting again when I leave you. Don't I owe myself a moment or two of peace?

JUDITH: If the army nowadays uses irony to defend us, no wonder you lose.

JOHN: You must be quiet, Judith.

JOACHIM: Let her be, John. This evening Judith is the first and foremost of our soldiers.

JOHN: Then she should know better than to make mock of defeat. She should stop treating us like a disease. Here's one of the defeated, standing in front of her. And I can tell her that a defeated man can see, thank God, how childish this everlasting blackmail is: women, honour, the nation's glory! Nothing lasts long in this base world: everything soon leaves us: joy, friendship, victory, everything except defeat. It is a man set free who is standing in front of you; the forces of the world, the delusion, the bloodlust, the self-torture, they have no hold over me any more. So in spite of the splendid heaving of your breast, O woman I have loved, it's as useless to insult the conquered as to smile at the conqueror.

JOACHIM: And are you also set free from your God?

JOHN: Our God always turns His back on lost causes. He will be grateful if we deny Him, for not involving Him in our disaster. And, if I'm to understand you, Judith is still here to save His face.

JUDITH: Yes, she is here!

PAUL: You have said enough, John.

JOHN: Everything I have said only seems to increase her monstrous pride.

JUDITH: Is it a crime to have dreamt that the name of Jew should stand for a race of conquerors?

JOHN: The most beautiful of our daughters! . . . Look at her closely, Joachim! Dare to tell me that Judith's beauty is sacred or eternal! Look at her coursing blood, and the anger of her nostrils. She is nothing but a flight of passionate humanity. I'll bet you, in due time, Judith will be either too thin or too fat. Her beauty belongs to the moment only.

JUDITH: The moment is well timed. I shall be the most beautiful woman tonight; that I can promise you.

JOHN: Why don't you protest, you priests? We're committing a villainy against God, and a crime against Judith! Come with me. Let's go, without any preconceived idea, and search for the one the prophecy really points to. We shall find her.

JUDITH: Joachim has searched already. The next most beautiful to me has the face of a pug.

JOHN: And the next purest to you is a whore. O city and people, if we have to perish, let's perish honestly. You're not the virgin of the scriptures, Judith. You know it.

JUDITH: I don't know it any longer.

JOHN: Joachim: ask her where she was, less than a fortnight ago, at this time in the evening, after she left the hospital.

JUDITH: Where was I?

JOHN: In my arms.

JUDITH: In this defeated puppet's arms?

JOHN: In these arms, and under these lips, your mouth a slave to my mouth.

JUDITH: And then, no doubt, I yielded and became your woman?

JOHN: You're not as simple as that.

JUDITH: You hear him, Joachim, the example of an inoffensive friend who, on the strength of a kiss given at a dance, will come to make trouble between bride and bridegroom on the wedding-day.

JOHN: I'll say nothing, then, in the hearing of your bridegroom Holofernes.

JUDITH: Holofernes doesn't exist. The suffering and redemption which carry his name exist. If I go to him this evening, those are what I go to. Don't try to save me by insulting me. I am not the first woman who has borne her beauty and purity as though it were not for another man she was holding them ready, but for a particular moment of history.

JOHN: Yet Holofernes is a man.

PAUL: Enough, John!

JOHN: Holofernes is a giant. His hands, his fingers, every joint is gigantic.

JUDITH: Don't make me despair. You don't understand, the only way I can be strong is if I give myself up without

15

imagining or even thinking. You are one of those lovers that one can kiss and hold for one evening, can even love, but can never marry.

JOHN: So marriage is to be without compassion. What is the world to do with that kind of bodily traffic?

JUDITH: Or with self-pity. Here is my question: Is everything lost?

JOHN: Everything.

JUDITH: Nothing more you can do?

JOHN: Nothing. Holofernes will attack at dawn and destroy the city. Whoever is going to the enemy camp to save the people should make haste. It has to be tonight.

JUDITH: And I shall go. John, you are the only person who could have persuaded me. (*She goes towards Joachim.*) Now it is in your hands, Joachim. Do you still accept me?

JOACHIM: I accept you.

JUDITH: Be quite certain: you are the one responsible. Look closely at me again. Perform your office.

JOACHIM: Be at peace. You are beautiful.

JUDITH: No one has yet seen me without clothes. But you stand as surety before God and the people that all is well with my body; feet and thighs and breast—the breasts are a serious factor in history—

JOACHIM: Calm yourself. Your calm is necessary, too.

JUDITH: And you also promise that I am purer than any of the others. Because I haven't loved one man more than another, because I have loved them all and chosen none of them. Because I have depended on them all, without distinction, when I was unnerved in the dark or in a storm, depended on their strength and their care for me, because I have been faithful to my own idea of pleasure and unfaithful to every man who loved me, therefore I am pure and God has chosen me?

JOACHIM: He has chosen you. Are you ready?

JUDITH: I am ready.

JOACHIM: Empty yourself of your will, become part of God's action. You know what is coming?

JUDITH: Only, no instruction, Joachim, no advice. If you have thought of what I should do, keep it to yourself. What I am is the event which is going to happen.

JOACHIM: Good-bye, then, Judith. Wait until the moon is up. You have time for your prayers. Are you coming, John?

JOHN: Not yet.

JUDITH: Let him stay, for the relieving of the guard. (*Joachim and Paul go*.) Because that is what it is, isn't it, John? A change from the day-time to the night-time, from the brave captains to the women, from men retreating to God advancing. This night and God have both given me passwords: one dark, one dazzling with light. How is it with the men, with the handsome captain? He has nothing to say.

JOHN: Don't come near me.

JUDITH: What do you do and say when the one leaving the battle meets the one going into it?

JOHN: We avoid contact. Let go my hands.

JUDITH: Don't you for a moment look at each other, face to face, each with an immense tenderness, an immense pity, tenderness for the one who goes into death, pity for the one who moves back into life?

JOHN: Thank you for the pity.

JUDITH: Thank you for the tenderness. Now tell me the password.

JOHN: Can't you guess it? It's your own name.

JUDITH: Which gate should I leave by?

JOHN: By the postern across the road. The watchman has been warned. He will give his cry, and open the gate for you.

JUDITH: Where shall I find Holofernes' tent?

JOHN: To the north: directly north.

JUDITH: Is there a pathway, a track of some sort?

JOHN: No. Get on to the upper bank of the second stream you come to. Don't drink out of it. It is poisoned. Don't go in those shoes; the driest battlefield will have some sodden stretches. And take your cloak; a summer night has a heart of ice. Are you afraid?

JUDITH: The desert and silence have never frightened me.

JOHN: Don't count on either. Every few yards you will stumble against a sack thrown down in your way, it may be cold and unmoving, or may be still warm; dead silent, perhaps, or still whimpering. A battlefield calls and cries, dreams aloud and weeps; and, imperceptibly, it also moves.

JUDITH: Is it far to the tent?

JOHN: The way I've told you, about a league.

JUDITH: What else can you tell me?

JOHN: Nothing else.

JUDITH: You haven't told me how to kill.

JOHN: How to kill?

JUDITH: At one sure blow, with a dagger.

JOHN: How to kill yourself, do you mean?

JUDITH: No, no.

JOHN: Follow your own intuition. We don't have to teach women either love or murder. They find by instinct where they can strike either pleasure or death into our bodies.

JUDITH: How do you kill?

JOHN: That depends.

JUDITH: On what?

JOHN: On whether you have time, or whether you are taken by surprise.

JUDITH: I shall have time.

JOHN: Then go for the heart, thumb on the blade: strike upwards.

JUDITH: How can I be sure that I strike the heart? – What is it? Why are you angry?

JOHN: Admirable, these careful preparations for heroism. Would you also like to know how a young girl can look a crude giant in the face? Shall I explain to you how she can save the essential part of her virginity when she's forced to give way? Do you want a lesson in loving?

JUDITH: Yes: that would be useful.

JOHN: I have something more useful here at hand. (*He goes to the inner door.*) Are you there, Susannah?

JUDITH: Who is it?

JOHN: I brought a woman here with me, Judith, to save both

you and us. You don't know her: she's outside your sphere. This is my last request. Listen to her.

JUDITH: So nowadays the last request comes from the survivor?

JOHN: See this woman. I'll wait outside. Come in, Susannah!

He opens the door, admitting Susannah. Exit John.

JUDITH: Who are you?

SUSANNAH: A friend.

JUDITH: I'm afraid you have come at a bad time. This is no day for friendship.

SUSANNAH: A woman who admires you.

JUDITH: No day for admiration either.

SUSANNAH: A woman who leads a life the opposite of yours.

JUDITH: In what way?

SUSANNAH: I have lovers. I give myself. I sell myself. Mine is the best known of the names that should not be known.

JUDITH: Then you have the right to speak to me this evening. What do you want?

SUSANNAH: To save you.

JUDITH: To save the one who is saving the city. Humility, I see, isn't part of your business.

SUSANNAH: Am I beautiful, Judith?

JUDITH: For the sake of your profession, I hope so.

SUSANNAH: Please look at me. What do you see?

JUDITH: Nothing that concerns me.

SUSANNAH: But yet look at me, Judith. I have something of your own beauty. My beauty, I know, is only on the surface. But yet I have something of your beauty. I have been told so a hundred times. I am your own height. And my voice . . .

JUDITH: Your voice?

SUSANNAH: It's true it doesn't contain, as yours does, any thought or depth of silence. But it is your voice.

JUDITH: You have been told so a hundred times. What man told you so?

SUSANNAH: What man? Scores of men. Every man who has had you in his arms, by moonlight or firelight. The man who swam two hours in the sea to tow away the wreck of an old boat you were tired of seeing: the man whose palm you suddenly kissed when you were drinking out of his cup, while you were watching the harvesters dancing, and left the mark of the red wine on his hand: all the men who came into the shadow of your longing, and then were roughly thrown off: all those who took refuge in my arms, either to forget or be revenged, and in between sobs and lovemaking called me Judith.

JUDITH: It's their password, today as well.

SUSANNAH: Every day, for a year, I've been secretly adding to the resemblance between us. I have brushed against you to make you speak to me, so that I could hear your voice. I have copied your clothes. Not so that I should please your friends. But as though I were your slave. Each time we met, even if only a day had passed, I felt outdistanced by you already. By comparison I was feeble, dull and poor, but I had the excitement of feeling led on to the limit of my strength, and wealth, and wit. I am like you, Judith.

JUDITH: In no way.

SUSANNAH: You are wrong.

JUDITH: Speak as I do, then – frankly.

SUSANNAH: I want to go instead of you.

JUDITH: I was waiting for that.

SUSANNAH: I don't believe the prophets. Most of them are enemy spies. A good many people think that Holofernes has heard the praises of Judith and is drawing her into a trap.

JUDITH: Suppose that were so? And suppose God had given him that thought to destroy him?

SUSANNAH: Holofernes is a barbarian. He won't know the difference between a disguise of beauty and beauty itself. Why should he, when so many men who know us both have gladly been deceived?

JUDITH: And God? Will God be deceived?

SUSANNAH: God has less passion than Judith has.

JUDITH: And to make the exchange complete am I to take your place beside the lover who won't know the difference?

SUSANNAH: You won't put me off with words. I'm too sure of my cause. I'm not concerned with saving your life. I know that you're not afraid. I'm concerned with something else. Let me go there instead of you. Tomorrow morning the people will think you have come back and everything will be safe.

JUDITH: What do you mean – everything?

SUSANNAH: You know what I mean – your purity.

JUDITH: My purity. So you use the fine words, too. But John certainly brought you here for a more realistic purpose. You mean to say my virginity.

SUSANNAH: I've given all my possessions to the poor. My home tonight is over there, with the enemy. My profession, for once in a way, will be to my honour.

JUDITH: My virginity? Isn't that necessary? And isn't it just that which you're lacking? Or have you valued it so much, in contrast to your own ways, that you long for it not to be lost?

SUSANNAH: Oh! Judith, it's not only our condition which alters when we become women: it's as though we change our sex and our species. And I want to preserve this miracle, the young girl Judith.

JUDITH: So the fallen ones are concerned about my virginity. I don't know what yours was like, but I begin to know mine. It isn't innocence, not even purity. It is a promise, carried in me like a child, the promise of a most wonderful defeat, a shame of great stature. God is transforming it into the promise of victory.

SUSANNAH: Judith, save Judith.

JUDITH: Who has said that I won't save her? I'm not going there as a willing victim, you needn't think so.

SUSANNAH: A weak, unarmed girl!

JUDITH: Every weapon, known and secret, I shall have them all. And the weapon most dangerous to Holofernes I have already.

SUSANNAH: Poison?

JUDITH: Not exactly. My tongue. Men are talkers. I shall stand there, a subtle girl in front of a savage general, a city's ambassador in the presence of a conqueror. Above all, a child in the temple, ready to answer a series of questions, what they will be I don't know, but only I have the answers. Before now I've convinced the most stubborn with a phrase, and confounded the frenzied passion of men. With a word and a smile. Tonight the smile may triumph. If I must, I shall smile . . . Why are you crying?

SUSANNAH: So much gentleness and violence sacrificed uselessly.

JUDITH: My violence! Then you can't understand my torment any more than John or the priests can. I thought, being a woman, you would have guessed how it racks the spirit to see the people, and the army, even God himself, trusting me with this immense trust. For I undertook this mission long ago, alone at night, all through these anxious days. Why should God have wanted to lift me beyond myself and overwhelm me with glory? This God, who has all eternity to play with, turns and for one moment makes my purpose His own. As for my gentleness! There's little enough of that now, except the quiet of desperation. Whatever belongs to my gentle life, I take my farewell of it now. Come here. Yes, into my arms. Don't draw away. This perfume you use is mine, isn't it? This necklace is twin to mine. Good-bye, perfume and necklace . . . All the things I know so well, I take leave of them here, in you: even of myself, smooth skin, eyes, lips – better so, in a sister than in the cold glass of a mirror.

SUSANNAH: You have to be saved, Judith!

JUDITH: I have to go!

SUSANNAH: No, Judith!

JUDITH: Give me your dagger.

SUSANNAH: What dagger?

JUDITH: Give me your dagger. I felt it on you. I have no weapon.

SUSANNAH: Here, then.

JUDITH: And your poison.

SUSANNAH: Here.

JUDITH: No tears. They're a weapon I shall never take from you. What is this?

SUSANNAH: Some rouge and a comb.

JUDITH: Give them to me.

SUSANNAH: Are you going like this, without a cloak? Take mine. Do you mean to wear those shoes? It's a rough journey; there are streams and fences to cross.

JUDITH: I shall go slowly. I'll take my own time. (*She turns to the door.*) How do I look, tonight?

SUSANNAH: As you always do, Judith.

JUDITH: As I always do? That is a great compliment to other times. (*She goes.*)

Susannah calls John back.

SUSANNAH: John!

JOHN: Has she gone?

SUSANNAH: Yes.

JOHN: This is the time, then, for what we planned. Not a minute to lose. Do you understand everything I said? Repeat it!

SUSANNAH: I run all the way to the enemy camp. I find Sara.

JOHN: Forgive me for sending you to that old bawd. You know the short cut? (*Susannah nods.*) Sara hates Judith, ever since Judith turned her out of the house last month. What will you say to her?

SUSANNAH: That Judith is on her way. She will ask to see Holofernes. That Sara must intercept her and prevent her from meeting the king, even if she has to lock her up until daylight. There's a good reward. Have I got it right?

The sound of the watchman's cry as he opens the gate to Judith – a mournful cry.

JOHN: Perfectly. Good-bye. You have plenty of time to get there before she does. The way I pointed out to her is a difficult way to go.

JUDITH

At this moment the Prophet appears at the window.

PROPHET: Judith! Judith! Save us!

John drags him in, throws him to the ground and kills him.

JOHN: Well, you, anyway, are saved from tomorrow.

Curtain

ACT TWO

Holofernes' tent. Uri and Otta, aides-de-camp to Holofernes. Sara.
A Negro called Yami. Some guards.

As the curtain rises enter Egon, another aide-de-camp.

OTTA: Come here, Egon, come here! Sara's conceived an idea
for once!

EGON: About time. Our officers are getting restive, Sara. You
haven't kept us supplied.

SARA: I provide what I can get.

EGON: Exactly. To start with you gave us young girls, who were
eager and pleasant to handle, interested in whatever man had
them. But since the famine got hold of the city you've
brought us nothing but the elder sisters.

OTTA: Or the grandmothers.

URI: Or the mothers. I noticed one yesterday with a child at her
breast.

OTTA: They go for the soup like wildcats, but for anything else
they're as languid as October wasps.

EGON: Then your widows: either utterly blank and docile, or
else going to the other extreme, far beyond the demands of
any honest infantryman. So what's this new idea you have?
What have you got to offer us this morning, to celebrate the
annihilation of your city?

SARA: A superb entertainment.

EGON: We know your superb entertainments. Twelve nudes,
with all the flags of the nations round their navels. Nobody
is interested in that any more, except the War Minister.
Suggest something serious.

SARA: The funniest scene ever played by a Jewish actress, or
that ever will be, even if you killed them all tomorrow.

EGON: Don't you worry – we'll never get to the end of Jewish
actresses.

OTTA: Don't waste your wit, Egon; you'll need it all later.

EGON: What Jewess? Is she here?

SARA: She will be.

EGON: Does she look like you?

SARA: She is young.

EGON: A peasant?

SARA: No, a millionairess, and generous. For three centuries her banker forefathers have been lending, increasing and stealing money, to build a golden pedestal for this lady bountiful.

EGON: Why is she coming to see you?

SARA: She is coming to see Holofernes, not to see me.

EGON: What are you plotting with this Jewess? You'd better take care.

SARA: Her visit has nothing to do with me. With everyone else, but not with me. According to the prophets, the Jews can only be saved if the most beautiful and purest of Israel's daughters comes here alone to melt the heart of Holofernes. This is the one. And she is on her way.

EGON: A good idea. Plump, I hope.

SARA: You don't understand. What is it you hate in the Jews?

EGON: Their pride.

SARA: Can't you see, then, that is precisely what they're casting in your net.

EGON: Our nets have caught plenty before.

SARA: Do you think so? What is it you have humiliated in the past? Kings beating their breasts, queens wringing their hands, prophets daubed with dung and ashes. But wait till you see this girl! Here's the pride of youth. When she sweats or cries it's like the dew of the morning. You're a huntsman, Egon. You know how every young animal, the panther cub in the pit, the young fox in the trap, goes uncorrupted and virginal into death. So it is with Judith. She is proud and brave. The only thing which will break her spirit is humiliation. Can I bring her here to the tent?

EGON: If you like. The king is in the inner room, working or sleeping.

SARA: Otta, bring me the cloak. Sit here and receive her.

EGON: Holofernes' cloak? Do you mean her to mistake me for Holofernes?

SARA: Yes. When she arrives, trembling with apprehension, she will be full of the notion of being a queen in the presence of a king, ready to play Sheba to a new Solomon. So receive her as if you were the king.

EGON: Why me?

SARA: You know how to talk. I told you she was a virgin; that means she's a prattler. You are better able than anyone else here to make a fool of her, to lead her on to a display of terrified heroics. Think of the show she will put on for us when she suddenly realizes we're mocking her. And don't underestimate her. All the Jewish people have put their fate in her hands; they'll be spending the night on the walls, convinced that at dawn she will come out of the camp, leading a repentant Holofernes by the hand.

EGON: Instead of which she'll crawl out like an infant that's disgraced itself. All right; are we ready? Let me see you pay me the deference that's due to a king.

URI: Come off it, you old queen!

Assur comes in.

EGON: Is the woman here, Assur?

ASSUR: She is coming.

EGON: Why have you let a woman walk freely behind our lines?

ASSUR: A spy kept close to her from the moment she left the city. She walked slowly and deliberately ahead, without trying to get in unseen.

EGON: At which point did she come in?

ASSUR: Near the River Esau, where the Jews made their last attack this morning. She knelt down and drank the water, which was dark with their blood.

EGON: And from there, where did she go?

ASSUR: We led her through the prisoners' cage, where, as it happened, they were being tortured. Now she is in front of the Royal enclosure. She refuses to sit down, and asks for Holofernes.

EGON: Bring her in.

Exit Assur.

URI: What role do we have to play?

SARA: Very simple. All the rest of us have to threaten and insult her. Egon, on the other hand, has to pretend to be charmed by her, and, bit by bit, she has to seem to persuade him to show mercy to the Jews.

EGON: In return for a kiss, a simple kiss.

SARA: Congratulations on your courage! . . . . Here she comes.

Enter Judith. Egon and the Officers pretend not to notice her arrival, and continue to laugh and joke among themselves.

JUDITH: I am here, Holofernes.

URI: Who dares pronounce the name of the king? Who are you to ignore the law forbidding anyone on pain of death from touching the king – even with words?

JUDITH: The woman there can tell you who I am.

SARA: Oh, so you condescend to recognize me, Judith. Not so long ago you had me thrown out of your house.

OTTA: What brings you here? The same hysteria that brought the other women? Hunger? Thirst? Do you want a drink?

JUDITH: I have just drunk from the River Esau.

EGON: What does she say?

SARA: I think she means that she has just drunk water red with her nation's blood, to partake of their courage. It is what is called a symbolic act.

EGON: If you have gone to all this trouble just to perform symbolic acts, my black-haired beauty, you are wasting your time. They are never of any use, except centuries later, to actors.

JUDITH: May the deeds that were done in the past serve me today!

SARA: There you are, as I told you!

EGON (*to Judith*): These words will do you no good. You must know how many have stood before me, begging for their lives or the lives of others, with sublime words and affecting gestures. None of them have ever moved me. You have drunk water mixed with blood. You're perfectly entitled to do it if you want to, but there's no point in boasting about it. What is your name?

JUDITH: Judith.

EGON: Sara, who is Judith?

SARA: A fashionable beauty.

EGON: Ah! The fashion. Wonderful how women of society can even lead the fashions of misery and war. A virgin, is she?

SARA: In fact a virgin. No virginity has ever been so desired, or escaped so narrowly. But she is still a virgin. She may well have guarantees from the High Priest. Shall I strip her?

EGON: Touch her and I'll have you whipped. Beautiful, you must admit, and better fleshed than the others we've seen.

SARA: I suppose the greatness of the times nourished her.

EGON: We can give her plenty of food of that kind. Is she a princess? She has the air of royal Judah.

SARA: No; a line of bankers. Under her simple manner you can detect the highly-insured jewels and well-sprung carriages. She needn't prepare her appearance either for love or death. The money has crystallized her.

EGON: Don't excite yourself, Sara.

SARA: It's God's injustice that infuriates me. It is always the rich who are chosen for martyrs. Look at her body, permanently anointed with oil, flattered and adored. The odour of sanctity is nothing but expensive perfume. Anyway, here she is in your hands, ashamed and choked with fear.

EGON: There you are certainly wrong. I can recognize courage.

SARA: She is frightened, I tell you. You see how stiff and pale she is. Like the boss's daughter in the midst of the strikers. And she says nothing. Oh, the dignity of saying nothing!

EGON: Any more of this, Sara, and I'll give you to Yami. Judith, why have you come here?

JUDITH: I wanted to see a great king, face to face.

EGON: You see him; is he as you imagined?

JUDITH: I don't know what I imagined. But I know I came here despairing and now I have hope.

EGON: What gives you that? Some expression in my eyes? Something indefinable in my beard or my bones?

JUDITH: A quality of your voice.

SARA: Watch out for her flattery!

EGON: A human note, is that it? Trustworthy and direct?

JUDITH: No; but under the severity, under the royal manner, I can sense a pleasure in life, a kind of adventuring; a curiosity which is a promise.

EGON: Be careful. Holofernes has made promises a thousand times in his life. He promised the Queen of Aleppo he would spare her only son if she would spend a night with the common soldiers of the barracks. He promised the god of the Phoenicians to respect his cathedral if he would manifest himself. The Queen did as I asked; the god showed himself in person; but I killed the son and burned down the temple.

SARA: The Queen and that god were not Judith.

JUDITH: Neither were you then the true Holofernes, nor the king I am here to speak to tonight.

EGON: Tell me, young maiden of Judah, by what title do you come here?

JUDITH: You have just spoken it. Young maiden. Do you know what that is?

EGON: It's what Sara was once. What they all were who now earn the world's opprobrium.

JUDITH: Do you know what it is?

EGON: Everyone knows except the young maidens themselves. If you know, then you're one no longer.

JUDITH: I am the exception. I know what I am. And it doesn't alter me.

EGON: It is to be a future woman, preparing for all the contorted shamefulness which makes a woman.

JUDITH: It is to be innocent; to be innocent is to hope, to hope to meet one day, among the wretchedness and disaster of our time, true human greatness.

EGON: And you hope to find this here? Poor girl! In the camp of your conquerors?

JUDITH: Spare my people, Holofernes, and your name will be honoured through all eternity.

OTTA: You can always count on a Jew to drag in eternity. They invented it, as a kind of interest paid on every minute of good behaviour, a sort of spiritual investment.

EGON: Tell me, Judith, speaking seriously, don't you think I have heard every possible plea that can be made for the Jews? Do you think you're more eloquent than the moonlight shining on the walls of your city, or the agonized crowd who throng there? Do you think I am deaf? Do you think the wide silence of the battlefield, or the vulture's cry half choked by the human flesh in its beak, the indifference of the stars, the contempt of the wind, haven't already spoken in your favour? All these things are Judith making her supplication, and Judith is no more than all these. Why should your voice touch me more than they do?

JUDITH: Because it is the strongest. Listen to me, sire . . .

OTTA: Here it comes, the heroic moment we're in for! The favourite concubine begging the king for the safety of her people. I warn you, Holofernes, I won't be answerable for my African troops tomorrow if you refuse them the massacre they expect. The poor rations they've been having these past months can only be made up for by the taste of blood.

EGON: Speak, Judith.

JUDITH: Great king! I know how much I am asking when I beg you to forgo the slaughter. I am a nurse. I tend the wounded and dying every day. I come to you proud in our knowledge of death. If the war could see us as we are it would not want to annihilate us. But I know the only distraction from bloodshed is more bloodshed. I offer an alternative, blood that is fresh and unspilled.

OTTA: A girl's blood won't go far among all our battalions.

EGON: Quiet.

JUDITH: Have you heard of Zittosa?

EGON: The fair city?

JUDITH : So it's called, by those who call us "the dark city".

EGON : Certainly we know it! It was the winking of the lights of those two, the fair and dark, which drew us to Judea.

JUDITH : Zittosa is eight leagues from here, untouched, as fat and sleek with peace as a larva, crowded with eunuchs and Caucasian girls, and patrician ladies. Instead of our empty granaries and wine cellars, instead of our skeletons of women, you can give your soldiers bodies like ripe melons, treasure and stores of food, and you will keep the only law which war lays down, the punishment of security and the flouting of peace.

EGON : What do you say to this, Otta ?

OTTA : Very interesting, but we don't need Judith's permission. Zittosa will have its turn.

JUDITH : Not if you delay, even for a moment. Our Council sent them a warning this evening, to prepare themselves or flee. But if you attack now, I know the way through the mountains well; I will be your guide.

SARA : Bravo, Judith, there is your true vocation. You were born to destroy, not to save. If God has called you to persuade Holofernes to kill innocent people, then I approve – it suits you well.

EGON : Come here, Judith. The game is over.

JUDITH : The game ?

EGON : I've been lying to you, Judith. I was expecting you. I'd already heard of you, not only through this woman here. The war could only be brought to an end between you and me. Well, we have met, and the war is over. Otta! Send for the commanders. Announce our advance on Zittosa. You may go, Judith; you are free.

JUDITH : Free ?

EGON : Go swiftly now to your people; tell them they're saved. Yami will escort you . . . do you hear me, Yami ? And learn to know your enemies better. They're not always barbarians. Though you're desirable, I impose no conditions. Not only because we're short of time, but I haven't the temperament to please you.

JUDITH: Sire.

EGON: Am I wrong to think that? Could you, without distaste, bring your face close to mine and touch my forehead with your lips, as a leave-taking?

JUDITH: Yes, I could.

EGON: Come, then.

Judith, distrustfully, kisses Egon on the forehead. He immediately seizes her in his arms and kisses her full on the mouth, while all around burst out in cries of mockery and derision. Judith struggles and frees herself. She is in the midst of a circle of people and has a dagger in her hand.

She would have stabbed me, the bitch.

SARA: Where did you think you were, Judith, you stupid little fool? In your court of love, or your chapel? With your lovers or your priests? You have waded into shame. What a fine notion of Jewish intelligence you have given these soldiers, mistaking this man for Holofernes! The poor of the earth have got their revenge on you now!

EGON: Yami, you can have her.

YAMI: No.

EGON: Take her, I say. I give her to you.

YAMI: No.

EGON: You dare refuse her? You know the punishment for disobedience?

YAMI: Yes.

EGON: Do your duty, guards.

Yami is taken off under arrest.

SARA: How charmingly she kissed you! What delightful restraint and royal eloquence! And who was it she convinced? Yami! A poor brute who can't hear or understand. I hope it satisfies her. She convinced a slave; her vanity is saved. Give her to me, Egon; I have work for her.

EGON: We can deal with her here.

SARA: Call your people, Judith, call your prophets, call your God!

JUDITH: Holofernes! Help me, help me, Holofernes!

The curtain at the back of the stage parts and Holofernes appears.

HOLOFERNES: Take that woman away. Kill her.

SARA: What have I done, Holofernes?

HOLOFERNES: Mispronounced my name.

SARA: I was only obeying Egon! Have some pity!

HOLOFERNES: This girl can say if she wants to show you mercy.

SARA: Mercy, Judith.

HOLOFERNES: If she says the word, you will be spared. (*Judith doesn't speak or move.*) Very well. You will die.

SARA: You think you can kill the Jews, you ignorant campaigner! They will live, and their Messiah will come. And not because of this virtuous darling of respectability, but because of me, Sara, the bawd! You're not going to massacre them all tomorrow. Every day for the past month I've been sending hundreds of young boys and girls into a country whose name you will never know. Safely away from our city, they will re-people the nation, and spit on your name!

HOLOFERNES: There was no need to tell me. The caravans have been seized each evening, and the young boys and girls exterminated.

SARA: You shall die!

She throws herself on Holofernes, but is intercepted by the guards and carried off.

HOLOFERNES: Leave us, all of you. (*All go, except Holofernes and Judith. Holofernes stares at her.*) You would think they came flying out of the air. (*Judith is silent.*) Or nosed their way up through the earth, as soft as moles. At a time when a man least expects it, when female company seems altogether out of the question, a woman turns up, by the tunnels of the air or the tides of the earth, bringing with her a breath of sweetness or cruelty that he never knew before. (*Judith is silent.*) And that's the only conclusion I've arrived at after ten years of conquest. These living moments only come when you seem cut off from life. The philosopher, absorbed

34

in irrelevancies, the general existing in his maps, the banker buried in calculations, all weaving, unknown to themselves, an invisible web; and suddenly they hear a beating of wings, a struggling in the next room. A woman has been caught . . . . all that's needed to be done is to free her, very gently, using both hands . . . Where did this one, such a perfect specimen, come from?

JUDITH: Across a field of slaughter.

HOLOFERNES: How women go away, how they vanish out of my life, this I always forget. But I remember every detail of their arrival: the colours they wear, the kind of light they stand in, their teeth in the first smile they give me: how they make you believe their bones are made of ivory. Indeed, I believe it still! The woman who goes is always identical. But how different the one who arrives! As you are, Judith. You separate me from the others by a greater distance than I've ever known. If you wish, you may make yourself prepared.

JUDITH: What am I not prepared for already?

HOLOFERNES: Are you ready for love?

JUDITH: I've been mauled by your captain. I'm not worthy of love.

HOLOFERNES: With the back of your hand across your mouth, all trace of Egon will be gone. If you like we'll leave no trace of him in the world at all.

JUDITH: No, no! Let him live, and the mark of humiliation stay with me for ever.

HOLOFERNES: Nonsense. Next time you bathe your face it will have gone.

JUDITH: More's the pity. A fine thing, when a woman's dignity and faith have been destroyed, when her God combines with a bawd to jeer at her. I am all shame, Holofernes; I am burning with shame.

HOLOFERNES: Come here, I can banish Egon's kiss.

JUDITH: You can never banish the false kiss of my God. It covers my life.

HOLOFERNES: We'll deal with Egon first, then. There. A face as pure as the water of a spring. It seems to me there's no

35

trace there of any of the kisses young men must have covered it with. Only anger knows how to make a face look so untouched, betraying its secret.

JUDITH: What does mine betray to you?

HOLOFERNES: The secret of your furious anger and distress.

JUDITH: What is it?

HOLOFERNES: Gentleness.

JUDITH: Gentleness? Don't you feel a dagger under my robe?

HOLOFERNES: I can feel it hard against me, like part of your body. Do you think I am such a greenhorn that I can't feel your body suddenly relenting in my arms? You are surrender, offered on the dagger's point.

JUDITH: Surrender to shame.

HOLOFERNES: You know as well as I do that human beings can only regain a lost foothold by emptying themselves of everything except the sensation of life. This you seek. Do you want it?

JUDITH: And when I regain my foothold, what do I feel? The old self-contempt and humiliation! My God and my people have spent twenty years flattering and idolizing me, only to send me into this ambush here.

HOLOFERNES: You came here to see me. Here I am. You wanted to speak to me. I am listening. What do you ask of me?

JUDITH: Nothing. Nothing else.

HOLOFERNES: You don't want to talk to me about your God?

JUDITH: Let Him speak for Himself, if He will. He has the power.

HOLOFERNES: And yet your intervention might be useful to Him. From what I know of myself, my sympathies would incline more to a weaker god, a god who finds men necessary to his divinity. What about your people? When you left them a few hours ago, didn't you mean to work their salvation?

JUDITH: It's a thousand years since I left them.

HOLOFERNES: They're still living; they still cry out – listen to them. They can be heard from here, calling to you.

JUDITH: I don't understand them any more. I'm ashamed I

ever spoke their language. Yes, they are singing. I know the song by heart. My innocence is a lamb, my courage is a tiger. The breath of God fills their words like the wind in a ship's sail, but now it's all intolerable. I have nothing to say.

HOLOFERNES: No, no, come now. Speak. You risk nothing here in this tent.

JUDITH: I don't understand.

HOLOFERNES: I think you do. You're beginning to guess where you are.

JUDITH: Where am I?

HOLOFERNES: Where do you feel you are?

JUDITH: In exile, on a bare island.

HOLOFERNES: You see, you have guessed.

JUDITH: What have I guessed?

HOLOFERNES: That here there is no god.

JUDITH: Here? Where do you mean?

HOLOFERNES: These few yards that surround us. This is one of the rare places of life that are really free. Our poor universe is infested with gods. From Greece to the Indies, from north to south, there isn't a country where they don't swarm, each god with his own individual vices and smell. The world's atmosphere, for those of us who like to breathe, is a hothouse of gods. But there are still some places that keep them out, and I alone know where. They are in the plains and on the mountains, like patches of an earthly paradise. Even the insects who live there are free of original sin. In these places I pitch my tent. By chance, and the accent of the palm trees and the voice of the waters, I recognized that this spot, directly opposite the city of your God, was one of them. So, for one night, I offer you the hospitality of this island, set in a pure and windless ocean. Put aside your intuitions of God, and come with me. I see that you're beginning to guess who I am, also.

JUDITH: Who are you?

HOLOFERNES: What only the king of kings can let himself be in this age of gods; a man completely of this world. The first, it may be. I'm the disciple of colour, and metal, and glory;

of the bursting fruit, and the sounding gong, of the towering wall and the rearing horse, of the storm that breaks and the rain that drums on the rivers. What are you doing surrounded by psalm-singing men, you entrancing child? Consider the charm of a day free of all terrors and prayers. Think of breaking your fast without the threat of hell, of walking the afternoon without a sense of sin. Think of young men and women simply in each other's arms between lamb-white sheets, without devils or disapproving angels. Think of mankind entirely innocent.

JUDITH: You offer me this innocence, only for as long as the night lasts?

HOLOFERNES: Such a gift is not to be despised. I offer you simpleness and peace for as long as you please. I offer you a child's world, the bobbing cherry with no worm in its heart. I offer you the music of the earth, singing, not sighing. I offer you pleasure. Under the blue sky of that word, Jehovah, you will see, will vanish.

JUDITH: Jehovah will come back with terrible speed. You will have to make haste.

HOLOFERNES: I? Make haste? No, I shall contemplate what I have. There's no vision in the world more breathtaking than to see a woman suddenly stripped of her god, still shy and uncertain in her marvellous liberty. How beautiful you are, Judith, and suddenly how clear. Your body spells out its truth to me like a child learning to read. Judith, what do you wish for?

JUDITH: You know what I wish for . . . to lose myself.

HOLOFERNES: Your body is saying so.

JUDITH: I don't know what it says.

HOLOFERNES: It tells me it is tired, ready to collapse, unless some man lays it forcibly on the ground: that it will suffocate unless it is stifled by strong arms. It tells me it wants to be caressed, and adored, it wants to be touched by lips, by the palm of a hand, by a forehead . . . the forehead of a king. It cries out to be its own god. What do you wish for?

JUDITH: To be defeated and invaded like a city.

HOLOFERNES: Both will be given to you.

JUDITH: But not yet, not yet . . .

Assur comes in.

ASSUR: Judith is here, sire.

HOLOFERNES: What did you say?

ASSUR: A woman came to the camp some hours ago: said her name was Judith. I thought you were sleeping and asked her to wait. Now she insists on seeing you.

HOLOFERNES: Two Holofernes, and two Judiths! The understudies are busy today. What shall we do with this Judith?

JUDITH: I know who it is. Let her come in; you shall choose for yourself.

Assur brings in Susannah and leaves.

HOLOFERNES: Are you Judith?

SUSANNAH: Yes.

HOLOFERNES: It's as well you say so. No one would have guessed it.

SUSANNAH: I am Judith.

HOLOFERNES: What does she want?

JUDITH: To save me from you.

HOLOFERNES: Is that why you're here? To save Judith? Is she in danger?

SUSANNAH: Yes, a different danger from the one I expected, but even graver.

JUDITH: You thought you would find me on my knees, weeping in front of a barbaric idol.

SUSANNAH: I thought I should find a victim and an executioner. But I seem to have interrupted an assignation.

JUDITH: That's true. One made by God.

SUSANNAH: Then praise God instead of blaspheming – for that's what you do: Holofernes is to your liking. Remember that our people think of you face to face with a minotaur; they're praying for you.

HOLOFERNES: And you believe she is face to face . . . with what? Doesn't every girl get the minotaur she deserves?

SUSANNAH: It's clear enough what she faces. The first man who has ever moved her heart.

HOLOFERNES: Who sent you here?

SUSANNAH: God sent her; a man sent me. But now God and man have changed places to keep us here. Help me, Holofernes.

HOLOFERNES: Help you – how? What am I supposed to save now?

SUSANNAH: The honour of the world.

HOLOFERNES: You mean Judith's virtue: is that it?

SUSANNAH: Today they are one and the same. While Judith is pure the world is, too.

HOLOFERNES: No doubt there is someone to take Judith's place. Nothing proliferates like a virgin.

SUSANNAH: You don't know her, sire. This humiliated girl here isn't Judith. I am more Judith than she is, though no more a pale reflection of what she was yesterday. Out of all our race, she is the only one now who is not Judith.

JUDITH: Those heroes who sent me out alone to what they believed must have a shameful end!

SUSANNAH: That was not God's thought.

JUDITH: I'm better acquainted with God, I think, than you are. His only concern is with the broadest issues. He wasted my strength of purpose on a crew of mountebanks. That's a proof that he needs my action, but not my support. A child could have told Holofernes from his servants, but I, the dedicated one, could not. God wishes to destroy me, so I shall destroy myself.

SUSANNAH: Do you hear that, Holofernes? Don't flatter yourself that you've seduced her. It isn't because she finds you handsome and powerful that she's willing to give herself to you. It's because life disgusts her.

JUDITH: You're wrong. It isn't life that disgusts me, but all of you, my own people, who either encouraged me to come here, or tried to dissuade me. For, either way, you weren't concerned with me, but only with yourselves, with an image you clung to. I was to be worshipped or petted. Purity was to be sacrificed or rescued, but not trusted. Now I must trust myself. Go back to my nation and say so.

SUSANNAH: Hail, Holofernes, the only living man! Good-bye, then, but let him take care. She came here to kill Holofernes. She has a dagger under her robe.

HOLOFERNES: We spoke of it not long ago. We know what it is.

JUDITH: Don't go near her. She has a dagger as well. You may kill us tomorrow, if you want to avenge me, but today my blood is my own.

SUSANNAH: Choose your own wound, then. (*Exit Susannah.*)

HOLOFERNES: Jewess, my arms are waiting for you.

JUDITH: The Jewess is here.

HOLOFERNES: The word doesn't offend you?

JUDITH: King though you are, it makes me your equal.

HOLOFERNES: Even though it conveys to people slovenliness and greed, the extremes of servility and ambition.

JUDITH: Also generosity and courage, as great as any in the world. God lives in his own people.

HOLOFERNES: And that draws on you the world's malediction.

JUDITH: God has never found a way of choosing a people or an individual except by suffering. One day He will learn how to smile, and the Jewish people will be blessed.

HOLOFERNES: Excellent answers. What remarkable domestic debates your future husband will have, if you stay alive.

JUDITH: That's another matter. It isn't your concern. I've already decided.

HOLOFERNES: Do you mean to kill yourself because I take your virginity?

JUDITH: My virginity? It doesn't exist.

HOLOFERNES: Why lie about it?

JUDITH: Almost at the very moment of coming here, I gave myself to the man I love.

HOLOFERNES: Nonsense. Why lie? You love nobody. Yesterday you loved mankind in the lump. Today you detest it in every particular. And anyway, women like you don't give themselves the first time for love; they give way to force, because they must.

JUDITH: There is no other force but God's.

HOLOFERNES: Undoubtedly. And God delegates His power to lusters, intriguers and captives of the host. I have been a substitute for God many times in that capacity.

JUDITH: On this occasion you're in for a surprise.

HOLOFERNES: Not a chance of it. A woman is a creature who has found her nature; you are still looking for yours; a virgin, therefore.

JUDITH: My nature is to seek.

HOLOFERNES: That is not true. You won't know until tomorrow whether you are mean or extravagant, an angel or a bitch. You will get up from my bed with your first child, yourself. What a marvellous surprise it would be if Judith, waking as a woman, was gentle and submissive.

JUDITH: I wouldn't count on it, if I were you.

HOLOFERNES: Suppose all the Hebrew litanies, with their hills leaping like lambs and their mountains rearing like bulls, could be changed to one word, lovingly spoken – Holofernes . . .

JUDITH: It's too heavy a name to be spoken so.

HOLOFERNES: And yet, not long ago, it rang out from your lips. Why did you call to me for help, instead of your God?

JUDITH: To match my feelings then, the only help was a man.

HOLOFERNES: And so at last I heard what I had never heard before: my name pronounced as if it were a sanctuary, or a password. You cried out, like a drowning woman, for a strong swimmer to save her.

JUDITH: What do you save me from now?

HOLOFERNES: From everything that would have corrupted you: from the dreary marriage bed, from waking in the bosom of a respected family, from a life of absurd memories, the tasteless dregs of living.

JUDITH: And from love, too?

HOLOFERNES: You know perfectly well you are giving yourself, not selling yourself. Admit that if in the whole of my body one blemish had made you shudder, you would have found a way to escape my arms.

JUDITH: And on your part: if you had seen the least fault in me, would you still consider that our bodies were destined to meet?

HOLOFERNES: You mean that we please each other.

JUDITH: I mean that nothing will be spared me, that the duel of Judith and Holofernes has become a conflict between a dark body and a fair one.

HOLOFERNES: Struggle is all that interests your God. You may be sure that He counted on our complicity and not our hatred . . . Come, and keep silent.

JUDITH: How can a struggle know silence?

HOLOFERNES: Like this. (*He kisses her.*) Have you often thought of this moment, Judith?

JUDITH: Yes.

HOLOFERNES: You have often seen yourself at last in the arms of a man, as though he were the first?

JUDITH: Every day, every hour.

HOLOFERNES: Was it pain to sleep alone, to be the only one to know your body?

JUDITH: It was like a death.

HOLOFERNES: And now you won't wait any longer?

JUDITH: Not any longer.

HOLOFERNES: Because you have climbed as high as your life can go?

JUDITH: Because I am lower than I have ever been. God has abandoned me. I don't know why, but He has abandoned me. Perhaps I have been too proud of my virtue. He wants it to be thrown away, without the smallest merit.

HOLOFERNES: And also without joy?

JUDITH: And without profit.

HOLOFERNES: Don't complain. Of all girls you are the one who is carrying out her mission. You will come to understand that presently. Young girls are created for the giants, marvellous or terrible, whichever it may be; but they are given to mere men. That is what destroys their lives.

JUDITH: It is what is glorifying mine.

Pause.

43

HOLOFERNES: Is there anything you want before you come to me, Judith? Are you hungry, or thirsty?

JUDITH: Is there no other woman here?

HOLOFERNES: At this time of the evening there will only be Daria. She will help you to undress. But don't expect to speak to her, or to understand her. She is deaf and dumb.

JUDITH: Deaf, dumb or blind, let her come in.

HOLOFERNES: I will send her to you.

Holofernes goes out, and Daria enters.

JUDITH: Is it you, is it Daria? Yes, yes, I know you are deaf and dumb . . . It is all over, Daria. No woman's voice will ever again call Judith the young maiden. What do I want? Nothing, Daria, except a moment or two with a woman. All the better that you are dumb. Your dumbness will be your chastity. For what crimes and outrages against men and God you must have seen; but your silence tells me that you are a woman, that you have been a maid, that you have wept and suffered . . . No, I'm not cold, thank you . . . You are deaf, and that's a good thing. For me, you can hear perfectly. I can tell you all that I wouldn't dare to say to any friend or relative. No, thank you, I'm not thirsty . . . Suppose I resisted him? No; there's no longer any question of being defiled. It is God who has done that ever since He chose me for my purity. I am going to seem proud to you, Daria – to say something that I could only say to someone who could not hear me: I believe God is only concerned with *me*, not with Holofernes or the Jews. Under the cataclysms which upheave nations, and men in their millions, He conceals His obstinate intention to track down one solitary being and to lead her like a poor animal to its end. Do you understand, Daria? There is no history of nations. There is only the history of Judith, driven to her knees. In a little while the business of Judith will be over for Him. What do you say? Is Holofernes handsome? Yes, he is handsome, Daria. It's the same with me as with all women who have faith in themselves; I surrender in a dark place to a seducer.

Well, there it is. If he were as ugly as you are, Daria, perhaps I would try to run away . . . Ah, yes? It will be pleasant, you think? I hope so, Daria, I hope so. Somewhere, I suppose, between crucifixion and uncontrollable laughter. Wait just a minute. Give me more of your dumb counsel. What silence . . . When a king waiting on his appetite, and a girl awaiting her end, and a people about to die, and an army about to kill, make such a silence, I could believe that God, also, is deaf and dumb . . . I hope He will forgive me, Daria; and that heaven's vengeance will overwhelm those who inflict on us these shames and these pleasures . . .

She goes into the alcove.

DARIA (*sniggering*): Amen.

Curtain

ACT THREE

Susannah enters, sees Judith's dress, and picks it up. A guard is stretched out full-length on a bench, dead drunk. John enters cautiously through an opening; outside the tent we can see the first morning light.

SUSANNAH: You, John!

JOHN: Who else? The archangels won't trouble themselves again with Judith now, Susannah. A captain is all she can hope for. Where are they?

SUSANNAH: How did you get here?

JOHN: Sara escaped. She came back and revealed everything, of Judith's failure and how she betrayed us. She has turned the whole city against her. She brought me to this tent. Easy enough to get through; she drugged the guards. All of them dead drunk, like this brute here.

SUSANNAH: What have you come to do?

JOHN: Can't you guess? Where the woman has failed only the man can succeed. Are they together still?

SUSANNAH: Yes.

JOHN: Get Judith out here, if you can. I know her. Now she's no longer sanctified she will want to be accursed. She will call and cry to rouse the camp, and get herself killed to save Holofernes.

SUSANNAH: They are asleep.

JOHN: Asleep. You say that without a shudder. Yet you know what their sleep is made of. All our people, young and old, have lived awake through this night; the mark of her exhaustion is on their innocent faces, while Judith sleeps refreshed.

SUSANNAH: Not so loud. You are risking your life.

JOHN: And I have to whisper, in case I disturb this rest; and I do, in spite of myself. Judith's wedding-night! I can describe it. I've spent my night following it in my mind. By remembering the words she has spoken most innocently in

46

the past, and her most simple gestures, I could follow its horror with absolute clarity. Oh, Susannah, how wretched we are, you and I!

SUSANNAH: As she is perhaps.

JOHN: Our unhappiness is undeserved; we loved her. But she has only loved herself. Call her, Susannah.

SUSANNAH: But Holofernes will hear us, too.

JOHN: She will wake to the lightest cry. Already, maybe, she is awake, staring closely on to his face, now so far away in sleep . . . (*He calls.*) Judith! Judith!

Judith enters, and John hides himself.

SUSANNAH: Judith, is that you?

JUDITH: Or something like me. What is the time?

SUSANNAH (*drawing aside the curtain*): Look.

JUDITH: Morning. This belt of blood over the hills; the last owl bewailing the loss of darkness; the breeze ruffling the grass and the hair on the heads of the dead men lying there; no sign of goodness in a relentless world, except the dark footprint in the dew, and the dog here, half-heartedly wagging his tail before he turns and runs away. The sky bruised and golden, Judith shamed and happy. The dawn, they call it. (*She has come forward, and John, thinking he can pass unseen, has shown himself.*) It is John!

JOHN: Yes, it is John. (*He goes towards her.*) Has the night been good, Judith?

JUDITH: Brief.

JOHN: Virginity has gone. That is over for you?

JUDITH: Over.

JOHN: All our people know about your treachery.

JUDITH: I am glad. I was searching for a way to tell them.

JOHN: Do you know they have stoned your servants, wounded your uncle, burnt your house, and the mob swarms the street, cursing you?

JUDITH: I am not theirs any more.

JOHN: Whose are you then?

JUDITH: You surely know that.

JOHN: Someone who has been stronger than your God, and truer than your people, more tender and faithful than your friends ? Holofernes ?

JUDITH: Until death.

JOHN: That's not far off. It is drawing very near.

JUDITH: It is welcome. You can strike.

JOHN: My hands have a purer mission. But if you want to escape you must hurry. The Council is sending the keys of the city to Holofernes, hoping to move him to mercy.

JUDITH: What can I do ?

JOHN: They have sworn to punish you. You know them. Even if they risk being massacred here, they will find you first and kill you. They plan the worst of tortures for you, because you deceived God.

JUDITH: Which of us, God or Judith, deceived the other is something still to be known.

JOHN: You have become your true self at last. I approve what our people have done. It is right that everything belonging to you has been burned: all material possessions gone, everything except this body of yours. All that is left to you now is reduced to that, as though you were an animal to be hunted.

JUDITH: Then be brave and strike. Be the hunter instead of the soldier.

JOHN: And in there sleeps the other one, satiated, gorged with Judith. The first man you have known to be weary of Judith.

JUDITH: Satiated and sleeping. As still and silent as marble.

JOHN (*drawing his sword and going towards Holofernes' room*): God has delivered him up to me. (*He goes.*)

JUDITH: Poor John. He has understood nothing of what has happened.

John returns transfigured. He throws himself at Judith's feet.

JOHN: O Judith, forgive me. Put this dress away, Susannah. Hold in your arms instead this cloak which was round her last night. An eternal blessing on Judith's hatred!

JUDITH: Hatred ? What do you mean by hatred ?

JOHN: I shall be worthy of you, Judith!

He rushes back into Holofernes' room and Susannah throws her arms round Judith's knees.

JUDITH: What are you doing?

SUSANNAH: Judith, the saint.

JUDITH: Stand up. Why do you say that?

SUSANNAH: Because you have killed him.

JUDITH: Killed him. That is a murderer's word.

SUSANNAH: No; a soldier's, a hero's word.

JUDITH: That is what I meant.

SUSANNAH: There is no other word, even for God.

JUDITH: God's language is not very rich, then. If that is the only word, it should be able to convey why I killed him. Let there be no misunderstanding there. Why did I kill him, Susannah?

SUSANNAH: Because God turned your heart to hatred.

JUDITH: Hatred? Do I seem like one who hates?

SUSANNAH: With a hate unknown until now.

JUDITH: And you waited, expecting me to kill Holofernes, in a fury of hatred, at dawn, when he had made me his wife?

SUSANNAH: I waited, expecting Judith to carry out her task.

JUDITH: Judith to carry out her task! Judith was far away. It was when I had forgotten all about my mission and my people that I struck the blow. It was when I was going to kill myself, in contempt of all our duties and laws; for what was left of the world for me, from now on: on one side a people I have deserted and who hate me: on the other, a lover shut away from me, forgetting and betraying me in sleep: no Holofernes either . . . This was what the revelation of love had become. It had separated me from my own kind, made everything I was before quite worthless, and the future could never exist. There was nothing left, for either him or me, except a single act of oblivion, death for him and suicide for me. Is this the truth of God?

SUSANNAH: No, you are still alive.

JUDITH: I live because if it is easy to drive in a dagger, it takes more courage and strength – and reality – to pluck it out again. I am alive because I knew at any moment his officers would come in and kill me, and I was glad of that. I waited for death. Sometimes in the night I knew that I had answered his loving clumsily, and though my faults were light, and forgivable in my inexperience, yet I felt that only torture could punish them, not suicide. Then I heard you, and came out to you, and I lived so that I could tell you everything before my judges came, so that you could bear witness against all those who would want to make Judith's story a story of hatred, could tell them they lied, and that what died here was only two lovers.

SUSANNAH: You are wrong; you killed him.

JUDITH: Certainly I killed him. I fell asleep, Susannah, closed my eyes for a fraction of time, overcome with the kind of weariness which a coachman feels in the first morning light. But that fraction of time was my night and my sleep; and then I awoke. Yes, for the first time I woke at dawn beside another human being. Everything was already in the past, it was all yesterday. A whole uncertain, jealous future prepared its assault against a marvellous memory. To me, already sure of my eternal death, he inspired a great pity, so poorly protected by his ephemeral death of sleep against the threat of the coming day. How can those who wake like this each morning near to one they love let them escape and return to life!

SUSANNAH: You talk to make assassination bearable. But to the end of time, you will be the one who chose God.

JUDITH: I did not. Our people shall know everything, Susannah, either through me or you. Listen: people are coming. They will give me the punishment I want. Tell them everything I have said.

SUSANNAH: I won't listen to you.

JUDITH: After all, why should I need you to listen? How absurd I am. There is a man here. Wake up, guard!

SUSANNAH: He is drunk.

JUDITH: Drunk or not, he has an ear. Guard!

GUARD: I am asleep.

JUDITH: You are asleep, but listen.

GUARD (*stirring, half awake*): Who says I am asleep?

JUDITH: Wake up. This is worth waking for.

GUARD: A woman. Hurrah for women!

JUDITH: Do you know what this woman has done?

GUARD: What has she done?

JUDITH: She has killed your king, Holofernes.

GUARD: She has what?

JUDITH: Killed him.

GUARD: She has killed him. Oh, that's bad.

JUDITH: And do you want to know why? For love.

GUARD: For what?

JUDITH: For love.

GUARD: For love. Oh, that's good.

JUDITH: There, Susannah.

GUARD (*going back to sleep*): There, Susannah.

JUDITH: There. I have buried the truth in a sleeping man. It will rise up again, even though it takes centuries, and stand against the truth of the generals and the rabbis. I was just in time. They are coming here, isn't it so? Who will it be? Look and see.

Susannah goes and looks through the curtain.

GUARD (*in his sleep*): For love, she killed Holofernes, for love. What's her name?

JUDITH (*leaning over the guard*): Her name is Judith.

GUARD: Why didn't Holofernes kill Judith?

JUDITH: Don't worry; she will be killed.

GUARD: Oh, that's good.

SUSANNAH: Here come the people, the prophets leading the way.

JUDITH: I am content. In spite of their hatred, because of their fierce curiosity they will pause between one wound and the next to hear, detail by detail, what I have to tell them.

The Jews burst into the tent, led by Joachim and Paul.

51

JEWS: Glory to Judith. Let Judith be glorified.

JUDITH: What are they saying?

PAUL: Hatred has been victorious over Judith. We shall be saved. Fall at her feet, all of you.

SUSANNAH (*to Judith*): I beg you, Judith, don't speak. Take care of Judith, Joachim.

PAUL: Holofernes' allies are in revolt. John is running through their camp, holding up the head of the king you killed. They have come over to us. The last of the loyal troops are giving ground.

A JEW: All the supply wagons have fallen into our hands. When Judith gives permission, we can eat.

ANOTHER JEW: We have reconquered our wells. When Judith gives permission, we can drink.

A JEWESS: You are our bread, Judith.

ANOTHER JEWESS: You are our water.

JUDITH: Listen to me, people of Judea . . .

JOACHIM (*interrupting*): What are you going to tell them?

JUDITH: The truth.

JOACHIM: They have God's truth, history's truth; no need for yours. Soon the two truths will be impossible to separate. Listen: we can tell you your truth.

The singers emerge from the crowd.

1ST SINGER: For two days, Judith has worn her dagger under her robe. At every movement it struck her thigh, like the tongue of a bell.

2ND SINGER: And she crossed the battlefield. No moon had risen. To find her way she followed the course of the streams like a raging beast. But her rage was the rage of the Lord.

JUDITH: It was only self-love and vanity which made her go forward. God was nowhere near her.

JOACHIM: Be quiet.

1ST SINGER: And Holofernes had a dream, and he left his tent.

2ND SINGER: He turned away from his Damascus Queen, painted to the heart.

1ST SINGER: Away from his Empress.

2ND SINGER: Away from the Egyptian acrobats.

1ST SINGER: From the dancing girls and the Bengal tigers.

2ND SINGER: From the hundred Muscovites who have seen the sun at midnight.

1ST SINGER: And then he saw Judith.

JUDITH: It is all lies and fables. Holofernes was alone, alone like a priest.

PAUL: Hold your tongue. In your triumph, how can you remember what happened? Only Judith pleases me, he cried, only Judith is fair.

1ST SINGER: She alone is the balm.

2ND SINGER: She only the hollow of the hand and the valley of the groin.

PAUL: But she was poison.

1ST SINGER: Sharp steel.

SUSANNAH: And hatred.

JUDITH: You betray me as well, and lie. Listen to me . . .

PAUL: Go on, you singers.

1ST SINGER: He caused her to be stripped.

SUSANNAH: But God clothed her.

2ND SINGER: Clothed her with air and light, and Judith was veiled with transparency.

JUDITH: It is not true.

PAUL (*to the singers*): Let us hear you.

1ST SINGER: He made her lie down before him.

PAUL: He made her lie down before him. Is not that true, Judith? Dare you say that is false?

JUDITH: It is true. Yes, that is true.

PAUL: Do you hear?

JEWS: Let Judith be glorified.

SUSANNAH: But God suddenly took away his strength, and he did not touch her.

JEWS: And he did not touch her.

JUDITH (*who has pushed herself forward*): He did touch her, and she was so filled with him that no place remained in her, even for God.

JEWS: What does she say?

JOACHIM: Silence; all of you leave us. Judith wishes to speak to me alone.

JUDITH: Stay, all of you, stay here! I speak to you all. Forget your zeal for perpetuating falsehood in psalms. Listen to the Truth, to the true and simple words. It is true that a Jewess lay joyfully in Holofernes' bed.

JEWS: What is Judith saying? Blasphemy!

JOACHIM: You are destroying us, Judith.

JUDITH: And that bed wasn't the couch of the fable which your psalms invent. It was a real bed, with pillows and sheets, do you hear me, you young girls? The linen was white and cool.

A PROPHET (*who advances armed*): Vengeance!

JUDITH: And she drew the joys of the bed to her, and exhausted them to their last. And in the cold of the dawn she obediently drew the blanket over Holofernes as a wife would do.

JEWS: We are lost!

PAUL: Do we have to force you to silence?

PROPHET: Let her alone. Speak, daughter!

JUDITH: Having to choose between her people and Holofernes she chose love, chose Holofernes, and since then her only wish is to find him again in death.

SUSANNAH (*stepping suddenly forward*): I was the woman she describes.

PROPHET (*striking Susannah*): Be satisfied, then!

Susannah falls and is carried off. Joachim drags Judith behind him. She is dazed and silent.

JOACHIM: I tell you again: leave us, all of you.

PROPHET: Why should we?

JOACHIM: I have to arrange for Judith's return to the city.

PROPHET: Be quick, then! The children and the sick are waiting for her return before they eat and sleep. Don't make them wait too long.

All leave except Judith, Joachim, Paul and the guard. At the moment Judith's body passes the guard he mutters in his sleep.

JOACHIM: What are your conditions?

JUDITH: You mean, on what terms do I agree to lie?

JOACHIM: On what terms do you agree to live and keep your silence.

JUDITH: Do I seem to you like someone who will live, or who means to keep silent?

PAUL: You have become proud and sensitive since yesterday.

JUDITH: But God has not. I killed in another god's name, not His, but He is unwilling for that to be known. He will dissemble and take the credit for everything. He will even put up with my being His chief representative in the city, circled with a halo until I die, adjusting the truth for Himself afterwards.

GUARD (*in his sleep*): It was for love she killed him. That's good.

JUDITH: Do you hear him?

PAUL: Who?

JUDITH: The guard.

PAUL: Your ears are ringing. He didn't speak.

JUDITH: Yes. He told you how I killed.

JOACHIM: How you think you killed. However, it is unimportant. Whichever it is you have been, avenging angel or deadly scorpion, it is done. It has happened more or less as we wished.

JUDITH: Did you foresee how I should welcome it, my delight in it, my obsession?

PAUL: Spare us these confessions.

JUDITH: What have you spared me? Yesterday, did you spare me your details of a monstrous Holofernes? That's all your triumph is lacking, isn't it? You would like to make me swear that Holofernes was an inhuman beast: but I tell you the frankest eyes of our race were bloodshot and squinting compared with his. His body was smooth and shone, as though it were the only human word which truly lived.

PAUL: Yes, yes, we've heard enough.

JUDITH (*turning suddenly towards the guard*): What does the guard say?

PAUL: Nothing. He is asleep.

JUDITH: Why does he raise himself up? Why is he sitting up and staring at me?

PAUL: He hasn't moved. He is asleep.

JOACHIM: Quietly, Judith, I beg of you, and help us to the end. If there is the slightest disappointment, our people will lose heart. Already your hesitation is a wickedness, because you are hesitating between God and one whom God hated.

JUDITH: I do not hesitate. I have chosen. I have chosen against hatred.

PAUL: Take care; you drive us too far.

JOACHIM: You're out of your mind.

JUDITH: God would be glad if I were. He detests me. Since yesterday I haven't once felt His pressure or His presence. I expected Him to hurl me against Holofernes, like a young archangel, pure, strong, prophetic: but He made me a foolish figure with a bunch of soldiers: and it was Holofernes who gave me back my belief in myself. I had my God in childhood, I had Him in girlhood. If He deserts me now, so much the worse for Him. Ah, Joachim, I thought I was impervious to men; I was afraid my body would never answer them. It was Holofernes who showed me the truth, and I will be faithful to him. It is God that I'm impervious to . . . Why has he stood up? Why is he coming towards me?

PAUL: Who?

JUDITH: The guard.

PAUL: You are wandering in your mind. You can see he is still asleep.

JUDITH: Is it his armour shining?

PAUL: Hallucinations!

JOACHIM: Don't try to distract us. Think, you mad girl! Can you deny that there has been a miracle, which happened at your hands?

JUDITH: The miracle, as you call it, happened because of many vile, contemptible things. Only God's enemy has behaved nobly and well. A just God would have protected all that was innocent, gentle, and holy rather than have brought about such a miracle.

PAUL: Perhaps so, if God had been a young girl, but do you really think that because that would have been how you wanted it?

JOACHIM (*speaking at the same time*): This is beyond all reason. You are destroying every way of retreat, and cutting yourself off. Don't any more suppose . . .

The guard has risen and moves towards Judith. As he starts to move Joachim and Paul are cut off in the middle of their speeches, and they remain motionless, out of time, holding their previous gestures and framing the scene.

GUARD: Excuse me, Judith.

JUDITH: Who are you? Sir, who are you?

GUARD: Such respect. Why is that?

JUDITH: A light shines round you.

GUARD: You have more piercing senses than I should have believed. Many men speak of angels, but not many see the shining. Very well. That is what I am, an angel. Now it is between you and me.

JUDITH: Between you and me? Why, it sounds like a challenge.

GUARD: It is time for the trial of strength. We must wrestle, you and I. You see me as I am; and I see you as now you are, the named enemy of God, stripped like a wrestler. It's between you and me now.

JUDITH: I don't understand.

GUARD: You will. From the moment you left your house last night, tell me, Judith, has your body suffered the least hunger, thirst or natural need?

JUDITH: Why do you ask this?

GUARD: Isn't the answer No? Was there any mud on your shoes after you had stumbled across the battlefield? Did the thorns tear you? Weren't you still dryshod after wading through the streams? Do your hands bear any trace of the murder you committed? All your life long they will be white and innocent, and your body will bear no mark.

JUDITH: It will bear the mark of Holofernes.

GUARD: That is what you suppose. When you go back to the

57

city, let the older women examine you. What they say will surprise you.

JUDITH: Who gives you the right to speak to me like this?

GUARD: The right! What do you mean by right? Stubborn girl. All the heavenly powers who have walked beside you from nightfall yesterday have pitied and sustained you, and made a sanctuary for you with their wings. But you have forced them, one after another, to veil their faces and leave you. I am the only one who is left, and you make me wear the heavy, stinking disguise of this guard so that you should see me.

JUDITH: You are the only one? If God is speaking to me at last, through you, it comes too late.

GUARD: You think that God will speak to you! You expect God to speak to men and see them listening, like a dog to the voice of its master. But those He has chosen God anoints from head to foot; and last night He charged us all to hold you safe in His silence. As you made your way here we slipped into the bodies of the dead, to arrest their putrefaction. Rivers of water and streams of blood flowed at your feet soundlessly. The dogs bared their fangs, but did not growl. And you never for a moment felt that we were present in that corruption, present in those fierce mouths.

JUDITH: You who speak to me, why were you silent?

GUARD: This is Judith, first in the class, the chosen of God! We rose to the hills and held back the echoes, caught every sound, made a dumb world; and the silence has meant nothing to her.

JUDITH: You must forgive me, then.

GUARD: Are you listening now? Do you understand what I say?

JUDITH: I think I begin . . .

GUARD: Tell your people the truth; you may find forgiveness there.

JUDITH: What truth?

GUARD: That you killed God's enemy, as God in His hatred charged you to do.

JUDITH: You know that isn't true!

GUARD: Is it not?

JUDITH: Did you not see everything? Weren't you yourself my witness?

GUARD: You dare to say it isn't true! Let us rehearse the night from beginning to end. You came in, and he was already on his bed, was he not, leaning on his elbow, waiting for you. At one look you measured up the battleground.

JUDITH: I saw a bed; that was all.

GUARD: God hesitates to ask a woman to fight on foot. The broad breastplate of his chest didn't frighten you, in spite of its clasps of muscle. You put aside your clothes and jewels. You kept neither pin nor thread.

JUDITH: And went to him.

GUARD: You went to him. And we exulted because all your naked body was a weapon: sharp as nails and gleaming teeth: your forehead as white as the smoke of fire; your ears sang with the sound of a holy war.

JUDITH: No! What I heard from him was reality, what I received was revelation.

GUARD: That could be so. God doesn't mind if His ways and wills are transmitted through human bodies and gross flesh. They are His interpreters, the means to His ends. But God kept you in His love. God decided that Holofernes should in no way touch you, and He threw us across your body like a transparent cloak. And the angel Gabriel was your mouth, and Michael was your body, and I was your right hand. And all night it was the heavens which performed your surrender. And, at dawn, it made you wish to kill him.

JUDITH: To kill myself.

GUARD: To kill yourself, if you like. But there was really never any question of Judith killing herself. What God willed was that you should only sharpen the thought of murder upon your own pure flesh, to make the knife edge as innocent as you. Suddenly you were blind to everything except a shining circle on the sleeping man's breast, a narrow, brilliant circle, like the circle a child throws in the sunlight with a piece of mirror. There it was, on the heart of this man whom you thought you loved. You began to look at it closely, to be hypnotized by it, as though it were a target. Isn't this true?

JUDITH: Perhaps.

GUARD: Is it true?

JUDITH: It is true.

GUARD: We wept for joy to see this hatred rising in you at last, very small to begin with, like a bead of sweat, but it was soon to bite and flower like a cancer of sunlight. And we, the angels, quickly made ourselves like rivet and bolt, which kept you from drawing the dagger on to yourself. And then when you thought of putting the dagger's point on to the circle . . .

JUDITH: I wanted it to sting there, no more than that.

GUARD: To sting?

JUDITH: Now it is your turn to understand me. If I had taken poison I should have also made him taste something of that bitterness in his sleep, not so that he should die; only to see the wry twist for a moment on the mouth I loved.

GUARD: And when you thought of putting the dagger's point on to the circle we all leapt upon you, increasing your thought a hundred times. Didn't you feel us, Judith?

JUDITH: Was it you who bore down my hand?

GUARD: Like an avalanche of spirits! And than, he dead, you waiting childishly for death, unmoving, like a bee after it has stung, we restored sounds to the world again, but so magnified that you heard the spider shifting in its web, you heard the mole tunnelling under the camp, and the fieldmouse rolling its grain of barley behind the bed. Then you heard the human voice of Susannah . . . There you see, ungrateful girl, how God has glorified you! Rise up and go to your people to tell them it was God. It is time.

JUDITH: No! No! Spare me that martyrdom.

GUARD: What martyrdom?

JUDITH: If God wills it, I'll deny nothing. Only let Him spare me; or take me, take me so that I can give to death a Judith who is still gentle. He can't want me to become a symbol of hatred and murder for the rest of a long life to a whole people, if ever since childhood He sets His mark on me to be the symbol of love.

GUARD: Don't struggle against it. There has been love, indeed, in what has happened. But not in you. It was in Susannah. Susannah was love. Accept the fact: nothing will be left tonight of the gentle Judith.

JUDITH: O you who have no name, should I feel this great sadness at not being able to name you if I had lost all gentleness?

GUARD: God, in the long prospect of time, reserves to Himself the right and power to transmute the sins of men into good, sacrilege into holiness, lust into purity, crime into expiation, chaos into creation, discord into harmony. There is nothing that cannot be redeemed at last. It is a matter of how the light falls.

JUDITH: It falls on my distress and agony.

GUARD: Enough lamentation, or you will fail me. What shall I say, Judith, returning, as I am now, in disgrace? To convince and save you I have betrayed God's secret, and lost rank and seniority among the principalities and powers. Go. If it will give you any peace, tell yourself that there is a fallen one in the lower cohorts of the angels who thinks of Judith with compassion. But do what I say; otherwise, there, before the people, I must take shape again and wrestle with you to tear the lie out of your throat, throw you on to the ground, as the ploughman throws down the shepherdess.

With a swift movement he bends Judith's shoulders towards the ground. Then he throws himself on to the bench, and the drunken guard sleeps again. At this moment Joachim and Paul come to life again and complete their interrupted sentences.

PAUL: . . . he would change his ordinance towards her.

JOACHIM (*at the same time*): . . . that he condescends to appear to you.

They are both very disturbed. Judith comes to herself and looks at them, astonished.

JUDITH: You, Joachim!

JOACHIM: If he means to be hidden, impious girl, it's not for you to find out God's hiding-place.

PAUL: He has blinded you with His light. Leave it so. Remain blind.

JUDITH: Have no more anxiety. I shall follow you.

JOACHIM: You will follow us?

PAUL: Only to go back on your word and trouble the people with doubts. No, no. We don't leave here until everything is settled between us . . . What do you want?

JUDITH: Nothing; there are no conditions.

JOACHIM: No conditions from you, but from us. We have to protect ourselves against any chance of defection.

JUDITH: Name your conditions. I shall obey them.

JOACHIM: You will live in seclusion. No friend or relative shall visit you.

JUDITH: That will be simple. My shame and my glory leave me no other company now than God.

JOACHIM: If the words love and pleasure still live in your mouth, say them for the last time; spit them out before you take the supreme silence.

JUDITH: My mouth is dry.

JOACHIM: If you feel your body defiled, call the servants; be washed clean. We will wait.

JUDITH: My body is dry.

JOACHIM: From now on you will judge and choose the punishments of all evildoers.

JUDITH: Very well.

JOACHIM: You will decide who shall fast and do penance with you each day. Do you accept?

JUDITH: I accept. What has happened to me no one but I can know. Even to speak it is to change it. Let it be called whatever you will, heroism or betrayal, hate or love, virtue or sin, it remains itself, the moment of life in which I, and only I, exist. It has no world, or history, or guilt, or purpose. Judith has experienced Judith, and been fulfilled. Now you can use His name for your scapegoat or your saint. Whichever you choose, there is no one to contradict you.

PAUL: Then all glory to Judith, and let us hurry. All can still be well. Wait: let me put this mantle round you. It is black, as becomes the espoused of God.

GUARD (*drunkenly*): And the widow of Holofernes.

JUDITH: What did he say?

PAUL: Drunken belching; how can we understand him?

GUARD: For love. She killed him for love.

JOACHIM: Do you still hesitate?

JUDITH (*going to the guard and looking at him with tenderness and repugnance*): This guard's tongue should be cut out, Joachim.

JOACHIM: Agreed.

GUARD: Judith, her name was. And what a body! All night long, without interruption.

Judith places her hand on the guard's lips.

JUDITH: Killed by soldiers whose ears are stopped.

The guard rises.

What madness has taken hold of him?

PAUL: What does he mean, blowing you this kiss?

JUDITH: It would be better to kill him, Joachim.

JOACHIM: He shall be killed.

JUDITH (*after a last look at the guard*): Your procession can move off. Judith the saint is ready.

Curtain

Tiger at the Gates

Original title: *La Guerre de Troie n'aura pas lieu.*

First performed at the Théâtre de l'Athénée on 21 November 1935, and produced by Louis Jouvet.

First presented in London by Stephen Mitchell and Robert L. Joseph at the Apollo Theatre on 2 June 1955, with the following cast:

ANDROMACHE	Barbara Jefford
CASSANDRA	Leueen MacGrath
LAUNDRESS	June Rodney
HECTOR	Michael Redgrave
PARIS	Leo Ciceri
PRIAM	Nicholas Hannen
DEMOKOS	John Laurie
HECUBA	Catherine Lacey
MATHEMATICIAN	Frederick Farley
SERVANT	Mary Holland
POLYXENE	Margaret McCourt
HELEN	Diane Cilento
MESSENGER	Patrick Horgan
TROILUS	Peter Kerr
ABNEOS	Duncan Lewis
BUSIRIS	Wyndham Goldie
AJAX	Christopher Rhodes
ULYSSES	Walter Fitzgerald
A TOPMAN	Robert Shaw
OLPIDES	Norman Rossington
SERVANT	Coral Fairweather
SENATOR	Henry Milton
SAILOR	Howard Loxton

PEACE, IRIS, FIRST OLD MAN, SECOND OLD MAN, MESSENGERS, GUARDS, CROWD

The play directed by HAROLD CLURMAN
Incidental music composed by LENNOX BERKELEY
Décor by LOUDON SAINTHILL

ACT ONE

A platform on the ramparts overlooking other platforms.

ANDROMACHE: There's not going to be a Trojan War, Cassandra!

CASSANDRA: I shall take that bet, Andromache.

ANDROMACHE: The Greeks are quite right to protest. We are going to receive their ambassador very civilly. We shall wrap up his little Helen and give her back to him.

CASSANDRA: We shall receive him atrociously. We shall refuse to give Helen back. And there *will* be a Trojan War.

ANDROMACHE: Yes, if Hector were not here. But he is here, Cassandra, he is home again. You can hear the trumpets. At this moment he is marching into the city, victorious. And Hector is certainly going to have something to say. When he left, three months ago, he promised me this war would be the last.

CASSANDRA: It is the last. The next is still ahead of him.

ANDROMACHE: Doesn't it ever tire you to see and prophesy only disasters?

CASSANDRA: I see nothing. I prophesy nothing. All I ever do is to take account of two great stupidities: the stupidity of men, and the wild stupidity of the elements.

ANDROMACHE: Why should there be a war? Paris and Helen don't care for each other any longer.

CASSANDRA: Do you think it will matter if Paris and Helen don't care for each other any longer? Has destiny ever been interested in whether things were still true or not?

ANDROMACHE: I don't know what destiny is.

CASSANDRA: I'll tell you. It is simply the relentless logic of each day we live.

ANDROMACHE: I don't understand abstractions.

CASSANDRA: Never mind. We can try a metaphor. Imagine a tiger. You can understand that? It's a nice, easy metaphor. A sleeping tiger.

ANDROMACHE: Let it sleep.

CASSANDRA: There's nothing I should like better. But certain cocksure statements have been prodding him out of his sleep. For some considerable time Troy has been full of them.

ANDROMACHE: Full of what?

CASSANDRA: Of cocksure statements, a confident belief that the world, and the supervision of the world, is the province of mankind in general, and Trojan men and women in particular.

ANDROMACHE: I don't follow you.

CASSANDRA: Hector at this very moment is marching into Troy?

ANDROMACHE: Yes. Hector at this very moment has come home to his wife.

CASSANDRA: And Hector's wife is going to have a child?

ANDROMACHE: Yes; I am going to have a child.

CASSANDRA: Don't you call these statements a little over-confident?

ANDROMACHE: Don't frighten me, Cassandra.

A young Laundress goes past with an armful of linen.

LAUNDRESS: What a beautiful day, miss!

CASSANDRA: Does it seem so, indeed?

LAUNDRESS: It's the most beautiful spring day Troy has seen this year. (*Exit.*)

CASSANDRA: Even the laundrymaid is confident!

ANDROMACHE: And so she should be, Cassandra. How can you talk of a war on a day like this? Happiness is falling on us out of the sky.

CASSANDRA: Like a blanket of snow.

ANDROMACHE: And beauty, as well. Look at the sunshine. It is finding more mother-of-pearl on the rooftops of Troy than was ever dragged up from the bed of the sea. And do you hear the sound coming up from the fishermen's houses, and the movement of the trees, like the murmuring of sea shells? If ever there were a chance to see men finding a way to live in peace, it is today. To live in peace, in humility. And to be immortal.

CASSANDRA: Yes, I am sure those cripples who have been carried out to lie in their doorways feel how immortal they are.

ANDROMACHE: And to be good. Do you see that horseman, in the advance-guard, leaning from his saddle to stroke a cat on the battlements? Perhaps this is also going to be the first day of true fellowship between men and the animals.

CASSANDRA: You talk too much. Destiny, the tiger, is getting restive, Andromache!

ANDROMACHE: Restive, maybe, in young girls looking for husbands; but not otherwise.

CASSANDRA: You are wrong. Hector has come home in triumph to the wife he adores. The tiger begins to rouse, and opens one eye. The incurables lie out on their benches in the sun and feel immortal. The tiger stretches himself. Today is the chance for peace to enthrone herself over all the world. The tiger licks his lips. And Andromache is going to have a son! And the horsemen have started leaning from their saddles to stroke tom-cats on the battlements! The tiger starts to prowl.

ANDROMACHE: Be quiet!

CASSANDRA: He climbs noiselessly up the palace steps. He pushes open the doors with his snout. And here he is, here he is!

HECTOR'S VOICE: Andromache!

ANDROMACHE: You are lying! It is Hector!

CASSANDRA: Whoever said it was not?

Enter Hector.

ANDROMACHE: Hector!

HECTOR: Andromache! (*They embrace.*)
And good morning to you, too, Cassandra. Ask Paris to come to me, if you will. As soon as he can. (*Cassandra lingers.*) Have you something to tell me?

ANDROMACHE: Don't listen to her! Some catastrophe or other!

HECTOR: Tell me.

CASSANDRA: Your wife is going to have a child.

Hector takes Andromache in his arms, leads her to a stone bench, and sits beside her. A short pause.

HECTOR: Will it be a son or a daughter?

ANDROMACHE: Which did you want to create when you called it into life?

HECTOR: A thousand boys. A thousand girls.

ANDROMACHE: Why? Because it would give you a thousand women to hold in your arms? You are going to be disappointed. It will be a son, one single son.

HECTOR: That may very well be. Usually more boys are born than girls at the end of a war.

ANDROMACHE: And before a war? Which, before a war?

HECTOR: Forget wars, Andromache, even this war. It's over. It lost you a father and a brother, but it gave you back a husband.

ANDROMACHE: It has been too kind. It may think better of it presently.

HECTOR: Don't worry. We won't give it the chance. Directly I leave you I shall go into the square, and formally close the Gates of War. They will never open again.

ANDROMACHE: Close them, then. But they will open again.

HECTOR: You can even tell me the day perhaps?

ANDROMACHE: I can even tell you the day: the day when the cornfields are heavy and golden, when the vines are stooping, ready for harvest, and every house is sheltering a contented couple.

HECTOR: And peace, no doubt, at its very height?

ANDROMACHE: Yes. And my son is strong and glowing with life. (*Hector embraces her.*)

HECTOR: Perhaps your son will be a coward. That's one possible safeguard.

ANDROMACHE: He won't be a coward. But perhaps I shall have cut off the index finger of his right hand.

HECTOR: If every mother cut off her son's right-hand index

finger, the armies of the world would fight without index fingers. And if they cut off their sons' right legs, the armies would be one-legged. And if they put out their eyes, the armies would be blind, but there would still be armies: blind armies groping to find the fatal place in the enemy's groin, or to get at his throat.

ANDROMACHE: I would rather kill him.

HECTOR: There's a truly maternal solution to war!

ANDROMACHE: Don't laugh. I can still kill him before he is born.

HECTOR: Don't you want to see him at all, not even for a moment? After that, you would think again. Do you mean never to see your son?

ANDROMACHE: It is your son that interests me. Hector, it's because he is yours, because he is you, that I'm so afraid. You don't know how like you he is. Even in this no-man's-land where he is waiting, he already has everything, all those qualities you brought to this life we live together. He has your tenderness, your silences. If you love war, he will love it. Do you love war?

HECTOR: Why ask such a question?

ANDROMACHE: Admit, sometimes you love it.

HECTOR: If a man can love what takes away hope, and happiness, and all those nearest to his heart.

ANDROMACHE: And you know it can be so. Men do love it.

HECTOR: If they let themselves be fooled by that little burst of divinity the gods give them at the moment of attack.

ANDROMACHE: Ah, there, you see! At the moment of attack you feel like a god.

HECTOR: More often not as much as a man. But sometimes, on certain mornings, you get up from the ground feeling lighter, astonished, altered. Your whole body, and the armour on your back, have a different weight, they seem to be made of a different metal. You are invulnerable. A tenderness comes over you, submerging you, a kind of tenderness of battle: you are tender because you are pitiless; what, in fact, the tenderness of the gods must be. You advance towards the enemy slowly, almost absent-mindedly, but lovingly. And you try not to crush a beetle crossing your path. You brush off the mosquito without hurting it. You never at any time had more respect for the life you meet on your way.

ANDROMACHE: And then the enemy comes?

HECTOR: Then the enemy comes, frothing at the mouth. You pity him; you can see him there, behind the swollen veins and the whites of his eyes, the helpless, willing little man of business, the well-meaning husband and son-in-law who likes to grow his own vegetables. You feel a sort of love for him. You love the wart on his cheek and the cast in his eye. You love him. But he comes on; he is insistent. Then you kill him.

ANDROMACHE: And you bend over the wretched corpse as though you are a god; but you are not a god; you can't give back his life again.

HECTOR: You don't wait to bend over him. There are too many more waiting for you, frothing at the mouth and howling hate. Too many more unassuming, law-abiding family men.

ANDROMACHE: Then you kill them.

HECTOR: You kill them. Such is war.

ANDROMACHE: All of them: you kill them all?

HECTOR: This time we killed them all. Quite deliberately. They belonged to an incorrigibly warlike race, the reason why wars go on and multiply in Asia. Only one of them escaped.

ANDROMACHE: In a thousand years' time, there the warlike race will be again, descended from that one man. His escape made all that slaughter futile after all. My son is going to love war, just as you do.

HECTOR: I think, now that I've lost my love for it, I hate it.

ANDROMACHE: How do you come to hate what you once worshipped?

HECTOR: You know what it's like when you find out a friend is a liar? Whatever he says, after that, sounds false, however true it may be. And, strangely enough, war used to promise me many kinds of virtue: goodness, generosity, and a contempt for anything base and mean. I felt I owed it all my strength and zest for life, even my private happiness, you, Andromache. And until this last campaign there was no enemy I haven't loved.

ANDROMACHE: Very soon you will say you only kill what you love.

HECTOR: It's hard to explain how all the sounds of war combined to make me think it was something noble. The galloping of horses in the night, the clatter of bowls and dishes where the cooks were moving in and out of the firelight, the brush of silk and metal against your tent as the night-patrol went past, and the cry of the falcon wheeling high above the sleeping army and their unsleeping captain: it all seemed then so right, marvellously right.

ANDROMACHE: But not this time: this time war had no music for you?

HECTOR: Why was that? Because I am older? Or was it just the kind of weariness with your job which, for instance, a carpenter will be suddenly seized by, with a table half finished, as I was seized one morning, standing over an adversary of my own age, about to put an end to him? Up to that time, a man I was going to kill had always seemed my direct opposite. This time I was kneeling on a mirror, the death I was going to give was a kind of suicide. I don't know what the carpenter does at such a time, whether he throws away his hammer and plane, or goes on with it. I went on with it. But after that nothing remained of the perfect trumpet note of war. The spear as it slid against my shield rang suddenly false; so did the shock of the killed against the ground, and, some hours later, the palace crumbling into ruin. And, moreover, war knew that I understood, and gave up any pretence of shame. The cries of the dying sounded false. I had come to that.

ANDROMACHE: But it all still sounded right for the rest of them.

HECTOR: The rest of them heard it as I did. The army I brought back hates war.

ANDROMACHE: An army with poor hearing.

HECTOR: No. When we first came in sight of Troy, an hour ago, you can't imagine how everything in that moment sounded true for them. There wasn't a regiment which didn't halt, racked to the heart by this sense of returning music. So much so, we were afraid to march boldly in through the gates: we broke up into groups outside the walls. It feels like the only job worthy of a good army, laying peaceful siege to the open cities of your own country.

ANDROMACHE: You haven't understood, this is where things are falser than anywhere. War is here, in Troy, Hector. That is what welcomed you at the gates.

HECTOR: What do you mean?

ANDROMACHE: You haven't heard that Paris has carried off Helen?

HECTOR: They told me so. What else?

ANDROMACHE: Did you know that the Greeks are demanding her back? And their ambassador arrives today? And if we don't give her up, it means war.

HECTOR: Why shouldn't we give her up? I shall give her back to them myself.

ANDROMACHE: Paris will never agree to it.

HECTOR: Paris will agree, and very soon. Cassandra is bringing him to me.

ANDROMACHE: But Paris can't agree. His honour, as you all call it, won't let him. Nor his love either, he may tell you.

HECTOR: Well, we shall see. Run and ask Priam if he will let me speak to him at once. And set your heart at rest. All the Trojans who have been fighting, or who can fight, are against a war.

ANDROMACHE: There are still the others, remember.

As Andromache goes Cassandra enters with Paris.

CASSANDRA: Here is Paris.

HECTOR: Congratulations, Paris. I hear you have been very well occupied while we were away.

PARIS: Not badly. Thank you.

HECTOR: What is this story they tell me about Helen?

PARIS: Helen is a very charming person. Isn't she, Cassandra?

CASSANDRA: Fairly charming.

PARIS: Why these reservations today? It was only yesterday you said you thought she was extremely pretty.

CASSANDRA: She is extremely pretty, and fairly charming.

PARIS: Hasn't she the ways of a young, gentle gazelle?

CASSANDRA: No.

PARIS: But you were the one who first said she was like a gazelle.

CASSANDRA: I made a mistake. Since then I have seen a gazelle again.

HECTOR: To hell with gazelles! Doesn't she look any more like a woman than that?

PARIS: She isn't the type of woman we know here, obviously.

CASSANDRA: What is the type of woman we know here?

PARIS: Your type, my dear sister. The fearfully unremote sort of woman.

CASSANDRA: When your Greek makes love she is a long way off, I suppose?

PARIS: You know perfectly well what I'm trying to say. I have had enough of Asiatic women. They hold you in their arms as though they were glued there, their kisses are like battering-rams, their words chew right into you. The more they undress the more elaborate they seem, until when they're naked they are more overdressed than ever. And they paint their faces to look as though they mean to imprint themselves on you. And they do imprint themselves on you. In short, your are definitely *with* them. But Helen is far away from me, even held in my arms.

HECTOR: Very interesting! But, one wonders, is it really worth a war, to allow Paris to make love at a distance?

CASSANDRA: With distance. He loves women to be distant but right under his nose.

PARIS: To have Helen with you not with you is worth anything in the world.

HECTOR: How did you fetch her away? Willingly, or did you compel her?

PARIS: Listen, Hector! You know women as well as I do. They are only willing when you compel them, but after that they're as enthusiastic as you are.

HECTOR: On horseback, in the usual style of seducers, leaving a heap of horse manure under the windows.

PARIS: Is this a court of inquiry?

HECTOR: Yes, it is. Try for once to answer precisely and accurately. Have you insulted her husband's house, or the Greek earth?

PARIS: The Greek water, a little. She was bathing.

CASSANDRA: She is born of the foam, is she? This cold one is born of the foam, like Venus.

HECTOR: You haven't disfigured the walls of the palace with offensive drawings, as you usually do? You didn't shout to the echoes any word which they would at once repeat to the betrayed husband?

PARIS: No. Menelaus was naked on the river bank, busy removing a crab from his big toe. He watched my boat sail past as if the wind were carrying his clothes away.

HECTOR: Looking furious?

PARIS: The face of a king being nipped by a crab isn't likely to look beatific.

HECTOR: No onlookers?

PARIS: My crew.

HECTOR: Perfect!

PARIS: Why perfect? What are you getting at?

HECTOR: I say perfect, because you have done nothing irrevocable. In other words: she was undressed, so neither her clothes nor her belongings have been insulted. Nothing except her body, which is negligible. I've enough acquaintance with the Greeks to know they will concoct a divine adventure out of it, to their own glory: the story of this little Greek queen who goes down into the sea, and quietly comes up again a few months later, with a look on her face of perfect innocence.

CASSANDRA: We can be quite sure of the look on her face.

PARIS: You think that I'm going to take Helen back to Menelaus?

HECTOR: We don't ask so much of you, or of her. The Greek ambassador will take care of it. He will put her back in the sea himself, like a gardener planting water-lilies, at a partticular chosen spot. You will give her into his hands this evening.

PARIS: I don't know whether you are allowing yourself to notice how monstrous you are being, to suppose that a man who has the prospect of a night with Helen will agree to giving it up.

CASSANDRA: You still have an afternoon with Helen. Surely that's more Greek?

HECTOR: Don't be obstinate. We know you of old. This isn't the first separation you've accepted.

PARIS: My dear Hector, that's true enough. Up to now I have always accepted separations fairly cheerfully. Parting from a woman, however well you love her, induces a most pleasant state of mind, which I know how to value as well as anybody. You come out of her arms and take your first lonely walk through the town, and, the first little dressmaker you meet, you notice with a shock of surprise how fresh and unconcerned she looks, after that last sight you have had of the dear face you parted from, her nose red with weeping. Because you have come away from such broken, despairing farewells, the laundry girls and the fruitsellers laughing their heads off, more than make up for whatever you've lost in the parting. By losing one person your life has become entirely re-peopled. All the women in the world have been created for you afresh; they are all your own, in the liberty, honour, and peace of your conscience. Yes, you're quite right: when a love-affair is broken off it reaches its highest point of exaltation. Which is why I shall never be parted from Helen, because with Helen I feel as though I had broken with every other woman in the world, and that gives me the sensation of being free a thousand times over instead of once.

HECTOR: Because she doesn't love you. Everything you say proves it.

PARIS: If you like. But, if I had to choose one out of all the possible ways of passion, I would choose the way Helen doesn't love me.

HECTOR: I'm extremely sorry. But you will give her up.

PARIS: You are not the master here.

HECTOR: I am your elder brother, and the future master.

PARIS: Then order me about in the future. For the present, I obey my father.

HECTOR: That's all I want! You're willing that we should put this to Priam and accept his judgement?

PARIS: Perfectly willing.

HECTOR: On your solemn word? We both swear to accept that?

CASSANDRA: Mind what you're doing, Hector! Priam is mad for Helen. He would rather give up his daughters.

HECTOR: What nonsense is this?

PARIS: For once she is telling the truth about the present instead of the future.

CASSANDRA: And all our brothers, and all our uncles, and all our great-great-uncles! Helen has a guard-of-honour which includes every old man in the city. Look there. It is time for her walk. Do you see, there's a fringe of white beards draped all along the battlements?

HECTOR: A beautiful sight. The beards are white, and the faces red.

CASSANDRA: Yes: it's the blood pressure. They should be waiting at the Scamander Gate, to welcome the victorious troops. But no; they are all at the Sceean Gate, waiting for Helen.

HECTOR: Look at them, all leaning forward as one man, like storks when they see a rat going by.

CASSANDRA: The rat is Helen.

PARIS: Is it?

CASSANDRA: There she is: on the second terrace, standing to

78

adjust her sandal, and giving careful thought to the crossing of her legs.

HECTOR: Incredible. All the old men of Troy are there looking down at her.

CASSANDRA: Not all. There are certain crafty ones looking up at her.

Cries offstage: "Long live Beauty !"

HECTOR: What are they shouting?

PARIS: They're shouting "Long live Beauty!".

CASSANDRA: I quite agree with them, if they mean that they themselves should die as quickly as possible.

Cries offstage: "Long live Venus !"

HECTOR: And what now?

CASSANDRA: "Long live Venus." They are shouting only words without R's in them because of their lack of teeth. Long live Beauty, long live Venus, long live Helen. At least they imagine they're shouting, though, as you can hear, all they are doing is simply increasing a mumble to its highest power.

HECTOR: What has Venus to do with it?

CASSANDRA: They imagine it was Venus who gave us Helen. To show her gratitude to Paris for awarding her the apple on first sight.

HECTOR: That was another brilliant stroke of yours.

PARIS: Stop playing the elder brother!

Enter Two Old Men.

IST OLD MAN: Down there we see her better.

2ND OLD MAN: We had a very good view.

IST OLD MAN: But she can hear us better from up here. Come on. One, two, three!

BOTH: Long live Helen!

2ND OLD MAN: It's a little tiring, at our age, to have to climb up and down these impossible steps all the time, according to whether we want to look at her or to cheer her.

IST OLD MAN: Would you like us to alternate? One day we will cheer her? Another day we will look at her?

79

2ND OLD MAN: You are mad! One day without looking at Helen, indeed! Goodness me, think what we've seen of her today! One, two, three!

BOTH: Long live Helen!

1ST OLD MAN: And now down we go again! (*They run off.*)

CASSANDRA: You see what they're like, Hector. I don't know how their poor lungs are going to stand it.

HECTOR: But our father can't be like this.

PARIS: Hector, before we have this out in front of my father, I suppose you wouldn't like to take just one look at Helen.

HECTOR: I don't care a fig about Helen. Ah: greetings to you, father!

Priam enters, with Hecuba, Andromache, the poet Demokos and the Mathematician. Hecuba leads by the hand little Polyxene.

PRIAM: What was it you said?

HECTOR: I said that we should make haste to shut the Gates of War, father, see them bolted and padlocked, so that not even a gnat can get between them.

PRIAM: I thought what you said was somewhat shorter.

DEMOKOS: He said he didn't care a fig about Helen.

PRIAM: Look over here. (*Hector obeys.*) Do you see her?

HECUBA: Indeed he sees her. Who, I ask myself, doesn't see her, or hasn't seen her? She takes the road which goes the whole way round the city.

DEMOKOS: It is Beauty's perfect circle.

PRIAM: Do you see her?

HECTOR: Yes, I see her. What of it?

DEMOKOS: Priam is asking you what you see.

HECTOR: I see a young woman adjusting her sandal.

CASSANDRA: She takes some time to adjust her sandal.

PARIS: I carried her off naked; she left her clothes in Greece. Those are your sandals, Cassandra. They're a bit big for her.

CASSANDRA: Anything's too big for these little women.

HECTOR: I see two charming buttocks.

HECUBA: He sees what all of you see.

PRIAM: I'm sorry for you!

HECTOR: Why?

PRIAM: I had no idea that the young men of Troy had come to this.

HECTOR: What have they come to?

PRIAM: To being impervious to beauty.

DEMOKOS: And, consequently, ignorant of love. And, consequently, unrealistic. To us who are poets reality is love or nothing.

HECTOR: But the old men, you think, can appreciate love and beauty?

HECUBA: But of course. If you make love, or if you are beautiful, you don't need to understand these things.

HECTOR: You come across beauty, father, at every street corner. I'm not alluding to Helen, though at the moment she condescends to walk our streets.

PRIAM: You are being unfair, Hector. Surely there have been occasions in your life when a woman has seemed to be more than merely herself, as though a radiance of thoughts and feelings glowed from her flesh, taking a special brilliance from it.

DEMOKOS: As a ruby represents blood.

HECTOR: Not to those who have seen blood. I have just come back from a close acquaintance with it.

DEMOKOS: A symbol, you understand. Soldier though you are, you have surely heard of symbolism! Surely you have come across women who as soon as you saw them seemed to you to personify intelligence, harmony, gentleness, whatever it might be?

HECTOR: It has happened.

DEMOKOS: And what did you do?

HECTOR: I went closer, and that was the end of it. And what does this we see here personify?

DEMOKOS: We have told you before: Beauty.

HECUBA: Then send her quickly back to the Greeks if you want her to personify that for long. Blonde beauty doesn't usually last for ever.

DEMOKOS: It's impossible to talk to these women!

HECUBA: Then don't talk *about* women. You're not showing much gallantry, I might say; nor patriotism either. All other races choose one of their own women as their symbol, even if they have flat noses and lips like two fishes on a plate. It's only you who have to go outside your own country to find it.

HECTOR: Listen, father: we are just back from a war, and we have come home exhausted. We have made quite certain of peace on our continent for ever. From now on we mean to live in happiness, and we mean our wives to be able to love us without anxiety, and to bear our children.

DEMOKOS: Wise principles, but war has never prevented wives from having children.

HECTOR: So explain to me why we have come back to find the city transformed, all because of Helen? Explain to me what you think she has given to us, worth a quarrel with the Greeks?

MATHEMATICIAN: Anybody will tell you! I can tell you myself!

HECUBA: Listen to the mathematician!

MATHEMATICIAN: Yes, listen to the mathematician! And don't think that mathematicians have no concern with women! We're the land-surveyors of your personal landscape. I can't tell you how we mathematicians suffer to see any slight disproportion of the flesh, on the chin or the thigh, any infringement of your geometrical desirability. Well now, until this day mathematicians have never been satisfied with the countryside surrounding Troy. The line linking the plain with the hills seemed to us too slack: the line from the hills to the mountains too taut. Now, since Helen came, the country has taken on meaning and vigour. And, what is particularly evident to true mathematicians, space and volume have now found in Helen a common denominator. We can abolish all the instruments we have invented to reduce the universe to a manageable equation. There are no more feet and inches, ounces, pounds, milligrams or leagues. There is only the weight of Helen's footfall, the length of Helen's arm, the range of Helen's look or voice; and the movement of the air as she goes past is the measure of the winds. That is what the mathematicians will tell you.

HECUBA: The old fool is crying.

PRIAM: My dear son, you have only to look at this crowd, and you will understand what Helen is. She is a kind of absolution. To each one of these old men, whom you can see now like a frieze of grotesque heads all round the city walls: to the old swindler, the old thief, the old pander, to all the old failures, she has shown they always had a secret longing to rediscover the beauty they had lost. If throughout their lives beauty had always been as close at hand as Helen is today, they would never have tricked their friends, or sold their daughters, or drunk away their inheritance. Helen is like a pardon to them: a new beginning for them, their whole future.

HECTOR: These old men's ancient futures are no concern of mine.

DEMOKOS: Hector, as a poet I approach things by the way of poetry. Imagine if beauty never, at any time, touched our language. Imagine there being no such word as "delight".

HECTOR: We should get on well enough without it. I get on without it already. "Delight" is a word I use only when I'm absolutely driven to it.

DEMOKOS: Well, then the word "desirable": you could get on without that as well, I suppose?

HECTOR: If it could be bought only at the cost of war, yes, I could get on without the word "desirable".

DEMOKOS: One of the most beautiful words there are was found only at the cost of war: the word "courage".

HECTOR: It has been well paid for.

HECUBA: And the word "cowardice" was inevitably found at the same time.

PRIAM: My son, why do you so deliberately not understand us?

HECTOR: I understand you very well. With the help of a quibble, by pretending to persuade us to fight for beauty you want to get us to fight for a woman.

PRIAM: Would you never go to war for any woman?

TIGER AT THE GATES

HECTOR: Certainly not!

HECUBA: And he would be unchivalrously right.

CASSANDRA: If there were only one woman, then perhaps he would go to war for her. But we have exceeded that number quite extravagantly.

DEMOKOS: Wouldn't you go to war to rescue Andromache?

HECTOR: Andromache and I have already made our secret plans for escaping from any prison in the world, and finding our way back to each other again.

DEMOKOS: Even if there's no hope of it on earth?

HECTOR: Even then.

HECUBA: You have done well to unmask them, Hector. They want you to make war for the sake of a woman; it's the kind of lovemaking men believe in who are past making love in any other way.

DEMOKOS: And doesn't that make you all the more valuable?

HECUBA: Ah yes! You may say so!

DEMOKOS: Excuse me, but I can't agree with you. The sex which gave me my mother will always have my respect, even its least worthy representatives.

HECUBA: We know that. You have, as we know, shown your respect for instance to –

The servants who have stood by to hear the argument burst out laughing.

PRIAM: Hecuba! Daughters! What can this mean? Why on earth are you all so up in arms? The Council are considering giving the city a public holiday in honour of one of your sex.

ANDROMACHE: I know of only one humiliation for a woman: injustice.

DEMOKOS: It's painful to say so, but there's no one knows less what a woman is than a woman.

THE YOUNG SERVANT (*passing*): Oh, dear! dear!

HECUBA: We know perfectly well. I will tell you myself what a woman is.

DEMOKOS: Don't let them talk, Priam. You never know what they might say.

84

HECUBA: They might tell the truth.

PRIAM: I have only to think of one of you, my dears, to know what a woman is.

DEMOKOS: In the first place, she is the source of our energy. You know that, Hector. The soldiers who haven't a portrait of a woman in their kit aren't worth anything.

CASSANDRA: The source of your pride, yes, I agree.

HECUBA: Of your vices.

ANDROMACHE: She is a poor bundle of uncertainty, a poor mass of fears, who detests whatever is difficult, and adores whatever is vulgar and easy.

HECTOR: Dear Andromache!

HECUBA: It's very simple. I have been a woman for fifty years, and I've never yet been able to discover precisely what it is I am.

DEMOKOS: Secondly, whether she likes it or not, she's the only reward for courage. Ask any soldier. To kill a man is to merit a woman.

ANDROMACHE: She loves cowards and libertines. If Hector were a coward or a libertine I shouldn't love him less; I might even love him more.

PRIAM: Don't go too far, Andromache. You will prove the very opposite of what you want to prove.

POLYXENE: She is greedy. She tells lies.

DEMOKOS: So we're to say nothing of her fidelity, her purity: we are not to mention them?

THE SERVANT: Oh, dear! dear!

DEMOKOS: What did you say?

THE SERVANT: I said "Oh, dear! dear!" I say what I think.

POLYXENE: She breaks her toys. She puts them headfirst into boiling water.

HECUBA: The older we women grow, the more clearly we see what men really are: hypocrites, boasters, he-goats. The older men grow, the more they doll us up with every perfection. There isn't a slut you've hugged behind a wall who isn't transformed in your memories into a loved and lovely creature.

PRIAM: Have you ever deceived me, Hecuba?

HECUBA: Only with yourself; scores of time with yourself.

DEMOKOS: Has Andromache ever deceived Hector?

HECUBA: You can leave Andromache out of this. There is nothing she could recognize in the sad histories of erring women.

ANDROMACHE: But I know if Hector were not my husband, if he were a club-footed, bandy-legged fisherman I should run after him and find him in his hovel, and lie down on the pile of oyster-shells and seaweed, and give him a son in adultery.

POLYXENE: She pretends to go to sleep at night, but she's really playing games in her head with her eyes shut.

HECUBA (to Polyxene): You may well say so! It's dreadful! You know how I scold you for it!

THE SERVANT: The only thing worse than a woman is a man; there are no words to describe him.

DEMOKOS: Then more's the pity if a woman deceives us! More's the pity if she scorns her own value and dignity! If she can't be true to a pattern of perfection which would save her from the ravages of conscience, we have to do it for her.

THE SERVANT: Oh, the kind guardian angel!

PARIS: One thing they've forgotten to say of themselves: they are never jealous.

PRIAM: My dear daughters, the fact that you're so furious is a proof in itself that we are right. I can't conceive of any greater unselfishness than the way you now fight for peace, when peace will give you idle, feeble, chicken-hearted husbands, and war would turn them into men.

DEMOKOS: Into heroes.

HECUBA: Yes, we know the jargon. In war-time a man is called a hero. It doesn't make him any braver, and he runs for his life. But at least it's a hero who is running away.

ANDROMACHE: Father, I must beg you to listen. If you have such a fondness for women, listen to what they have to say to you, for I can promise I speak for all the women in the world. Let us keep our husbands as they are. The gods took care to see they were surrounded with enough obstacles and dangers to keep them brave and vigorous. Quite enough if they had nothing to cope with except floods and storms! Or only wild animals! The small game, foxes and hares and pheasants, which a woman can scarcely distinguish from the heather they hide in, prove a man's quickness of eye far better than this target you propose: the enemy's heart hiding in flesh and metal. Whenever I have seen a man kill a stag or an eagle, I have offered up thanks to them. I know they died for Hector. Why should you want me to owe Hector to the deaths of other men?

PRIAM: I don't want it, my dear child. But why do you think you are here now, all looking so beautiful, and valiantly demanding peace? Why: because your husbands and your fathers, and their fathers, and theirs, were fighting men. If they had been too lazy and self-indulgent to spring to arms, if they hadn't known how this dull and stupid business we call life suddenly leaps into flame and justifies itself through the scorn men have for it, you would find *you* were the cowards now, and you would be clamouring for war. A man has only one way of being immortal on this earth: he has to forget he is mortal.

ANDROMACHE: Why, exactly so, father: you're only too right. The brave men die in war. It takes great luck or judgement not to be killed. Once at least the head has to bow and the knee has to bend to danger. The soldiers who march back under the triumphal arches are death's deserters. How can a country increase in strength and honour by sending them both to their graves?

PRIAM: Daughter, the first sign of cowardice in a people is their first moment of decay.

ANDROMACHE: But which is the worse cowardice? To appear cowardly to others, and make sure of peace? Or to be cowardly in your own eyes, and let loose a war?

DEMOKOS: Cowardice is not to prefer death on every hand rather than the death of one's native land.

87

HECUBA: I was expecting poetry at this point. It never lets us down.

ANDROMACHE: Everyone always dies for his country. If you have lived in it, well and wisely and actively, you die for it too.

HECUBA: It would be better if only the old men fought the wars. Every country is the country of youth. When its youth dies it dies with them.

DEMOKOS: All this nonsense about youth! In thirty years' time youth is nothing but these old men you talk about.

CASSANDRA: Wrong.

HECUBA: Wrong! When a grown man reaches forty we change him for an old one. He has completely disappeared. There's only the most superficial resemblance between the two of them. Nothing is handed on from one to the other.

DEMOKOS: I still take a serious concern in my fame as a poet.

HECUBA: Yes, that's quite true. And your rheumatism.

Another outburst of laughter from the servants.

HECTOR: And you can listen to all this without saying a word, Paris? Can you still not decide to give up an adventure to save us from years of unhappiness and massacre?

PARIS: What do you want me to say? My case is an international problem.

HECTOR: Are you really in love with Helen, Paris?

CASSANDRA: They've become now a kind of symbol of love's devotion. They don't still have to love each other.

PARIS: I worship Helen.

CASSANDRA (*at the rampart*): Here she is.

HECTOR: If I persuade her to set sail, will you agree?

PARIS: Yes, I'll agree.

HECTOR: Father, if Helen is willing to go back to Greece, will you hold her here by force?

PRIAM: Why discuss the impossible?

HECTOR: Do you call it impossible? If women are a tenth of what you say they are, Helen will go of her own free will.

PARIS: Father, now *I'm* going to ask you to let him do what

he wants. You have seen what it's like. As soon as the
question of Helen cropped up, this whole tribe royal turned
itself into a family conclave of all the poor girl's sisters-in-
law, mother- and father-in-law, brother-in-law, worthy of
the best middle-class tradition. I doubt if there's anything
more humiliating than to be cast for the part of the seducer
son in a large family. I've had quite enough of their insinua-
tions. I accept Hector's challenge.

DEMOKOS: Helen's not only yours, Paris. She belongs to the
city. She belongs to our country.

MATHEMATICIAN: She belongs to the landscape.

HECUBA: You be quiet, mathematician.

CASSANDRA: Here's Helen; here she is.

HECTOR: Father, I must ask you to let me handle this. Listen:
they are calling us to go to the ceremony, to close the Gates
of War. Leave this to me. I'll join you soon.

PRIAM: Do you really agree to this, Paris?

PARIS: I'm eager for it.

PRIAM: Very well, then; let it be so. Come along, the rest of
you; we will see that the Gates of War are made ready.

CASSANDRA: Those poor gates. They need more oil to shut
them than to open them.

Paris and the rest withdraw. Demokos stays.

HECTOR: What are you waiting for?

DEMOKOS: The visitation of my genius.

HECTOR: Say that again?

DEMOKOS: Every time Helen walks my way I am thrown into
a transport of inspiration. I shake all over, break into sweat,
and improvise. Good heavens, here it is! (*He declaims:*)

> Beautiful Helen, Helen of Sparta,
>> Singular as the evening star,
> The gods forbid that we should part a
> Pair as fair as you and Paris are.

HECTOR: Your line-endings give me a headache.

DEMOKOS: It's an invention of mine. I can obtain effects even
more surprising. Listen. (*He declaims:*)

Face the great Hector with no qualm,
  Troy's glory though he be, and the
    world's terror:
He is the storm, and you the after-calm,
  Yours is the right, and his the boist'rous
    error.

HECTOR: Get out!

DEMOKOS: What are you glaring at? You look as though you
have as little liking for poetry as you have for war.

HECTOR: They make a pretty couple! Now vanish.

Exit Demokos. Enter Cassandra.

CASSANDRA: Helen!

Enter Helen and Paris.

PARIS: Here he is, Helen darling; this is Hector. He has a
proposition to make to you, a perfectly simple proposition.
He wants to hand you over to the Greeks, and prove to you
that you don't love me. Tell me you do love me, before I
leave you with him. Tell me in your own words.

HELEN: I adore you, my sweet.

PARIS: Tell me how beautiful the wave was which swept you
away from Greece.

HELEN: Magnificent! A magnificent wave! Where did you see
a wave? The sea was so calm.

PARIS: Tell me you hate Menelaus.

HELEN: Menelaus? I hate him.

PARIS: You haven't finished yet. I shall never again return to
Greece. Say that.

HELEN: You will never again return to Greece.

PARIS: No, no, this is about you, my darling.

HELEN: Oh, of course! How silly I am! I shall never again
return to Greece.

PARIS: I didn't make her say it. – Now it's up to you.

He goes off.

HECTOR: Is Greece a beautiful country?

HELEN: Paris found it ravishing.

HECTOR: I meant is Greece itself beautiful, apart from Helen?

HELEN: How very charming of you.

HECTOR: I was simply wondering what it is really like.

HELEN: Well, there are quite a great many kings, and a great many goats, dotted about on marble.

HECTOR: If the kings are in gold, and the goats angora, that would look pretty well when the sun was rising.

HELEN: I don't get up very early.

HECTOR: And a great many gods as well, I believe? Paris tells me the sky is crawling with them; he tells me you can see the legs of goddesses hanging down from the clouds.

HELEN: Paris always goes about with his nose in the air. He may have seen them.

HECTOR: But you haven't?

HELEN: I am not gifted that way. I will look out for them when I go back there again.

HECTOR: You were telling Paris you would never be going back there.

HELEN: He asked me to tell him so. I adore doing what Paris wants me to do.

HECTOR: I see. Is that also true of what you said about Menelaus? Do you not, after all, hate him?

HELEN: Why should I hate him?

HECTOR: For the one reason which might certainly make for hate. You have seen too much of him.

HELEN: Menelaus? Oh, no! I have never seen Menelaus. On the contrary.

HECTOR: You have never seen your husband?

HELEN: There are some things, and certain people, that stand out in bright colours for me. They are the ones I can see. I believe in them. I have never been able to see Menelaus.

HECTOR: Though I suppose he must have come very close to you sometimes.

HELEN: I have been able to touch him. But I can't honestly tell you I saw him.

HECTOR: They say he never left your side.

HELEN: Apparently. I must have walked across him a great many times without knowing it.

HECTOR: Whereas you have seen Paris.

HELEN: Vividly; in the clearest outline against the sky and the sun.

HECTOR: Does he still stand out as vividly as he did? Look down there: leaning against the rampart.

HELEN: Are you sure that's Paris, down there?

HECTOR: He is waiting for you.

HELEN: Good gracious! He's not nearly as clear as usual!

HECTOR: And yet the wall is freshly whitewashed. Look again: there he is in profile.

HELEN: It's odd how people waiting for you stand out far less clearly than people you are waiting for.

HECTOR: Are you sure that Paris loves you?

HELEN: I don't like knowing about other people's feelings. There is nothing more embarrassing. Just as when you play cards and you see your opponent's hand. You are sure to lose.

HECTOR: What about yourself? Do you love him?

HELEN: I don't much like knowing my own feelings either.

HECTOR: But, listen: when you make love with Paris, when he sleeps in your arms, when you are circled round with Paris, overwhelmed with Paris, haven't you any thoughts about it?

HELEN: My part is over. I leave any thinking to the universe. It does it much better than I do.

HECTOR: Have there been many others, before Paris?

HELEN: Some.

HECTOR: And there will be others after him, wouldn't you say, as long as they stand out in clear relief against the sky, or the wall, or the white sheets on the bed? It is just as I thought it was. You don't love Paris particularly, Helen; you love men.

HELEN: I don't dislike them. They're as pleasant as soap and a sponge and warm water; you feel cleansed and refreshed by them.

HECTOR: Cassandra! Cassandra!

CASSANDRA (*entering*): What do you want?

HECTOR: Cassandra, Helen is going back this evening with the Greek ambassador.

HELEN: I? What makes you think so?

HECTOR: Weren't you telling me that you didn't love Paris particularly?

HELEN: That was your interpretation. Still, if you like.

HECTOR: I quote my authority. You have the same liking for men as you have for a cake of soap.

HELEN: Yes; or pumice stone perhaps is better. What about it?

HECTOR: Well then, you're not going to hesitate in your choice between going back to Greece, which you don't mind, and a catastrophe as terrible as war?

HELEN: You don't understand me at all, Hector. Of course I'm not hesitating. It would be very easy to say "I will do this or that, so that this can happen or that can happen". You've discovered my weakness and you are overjoyed. The man who discovers a woman's weakness is like the huntsman in the heat of the day who finds a cool spring. He wallows in it. But you mustn't think, because you have convinced me, you've convinced the future, too. Merely by making children behave as you want them to, you don't alter the course of destiny.

HECTOR: I don't follow your Greek shades and subtleties.

HELEN: It's not a question of shades and subtleties. It's no less than a question of monsters and pyramids.

HECTOR: Do you choose to leave here, yes or no?

HELEN: Don't bully me. I choose what happens in the way I choose men, or anything else. I choose whatever is not indefinite and vague. I choose what I see.

HECTOR: I know, you said that: what you see in the brightest colours. And you don't see yourself returning to Menelaus in a few days' time?

HELEN: No. It's very difficult.

HECTOR: We could no doubt persuade your husband to dress with great brilliance for your return.

HELEN: All the purple dye from all the murex shells in the sea wouldn't make him visible to me.

HECTOR: Here you have a rival, Cassandra. Helen can read the future, too.

HELEN: No, I can't read the future. But when I imagine the future some of the pictures I see are coloured, and some are dull and drab. And up to now it has always been the coloured scenes which have happened in the end.

HECTOR: We are going to give you back to the Greeks at high noon, on the blinding sand, between the violet sea and the ochre-coloured wall. We shall all be in golden armour with red skirts; and my sisters, dressed in green and standing between my white stallion and Priam's black mare, will return you to the Greek ambassador, over whose silver helmet I can imagine tall purple plumes. You see that, I think?

HELEN: No, none of it. It is all quite sombre.

HECTOR: You are mocking me, aren't you?

HELEN: Why should I mock you? Very well, then. Let us go, if you like! Let us go and get ready to return me to the Greeks. We shall see what happens.

HECTOR: Do you realize how you insult humanity, or is it unconscious?

HELEN: I don't know what you mean.

HECTOR: You realize that your coloured picture-book is holding the world up to ridicule? While we are all battling and making sacrifices to bring about a time we can call our own, there are you, looking at your pictures which nothing in all eternity can alter. What's wrong? Which one has made you stop and stare at it with those blind eyes? I don't doubt it's the one where you are standing here on the ramparts, watching the battle going on below. Is it the battle you see?

HELEN: Yes.

HECTOR: And the city is in ruins or burning, isn't that so?

HELEN: Yes. It's a vivid red.

HECTOR: And what about Paris? You are seeing his body dragged behind a chariot?

HELEN: Oh, do you think that is Paris? I see what looks like a flash of sunlight rolling in the dust. A diamond sparkling on his hand. Yes, it is! Often I don't recognize faces, but I always recognize the jewellery. It's his ring, I'm quite certain.

HECTOR: Exactly. Do I dare to ask you about Andromache, and myself, the scene of Andromache and Hector? You are looking at us. Don't deny it. How do you see us? Happy, grown old, bathed in light?

HELEN: I am not trying to see it.

HECTOR: The scene of Andromache weeping over the body of Hector, does that shine clearer?

HELEN: You seem to know. But sometimes I see things shining, brilliantly shining, and they never happen. No one is infallible.

HECTOR: You needn't go on. I understand. There is a son between the weeping mother and the father stretched on the ground?

HELEN: Yes. He is playing with his father's tangled hair. He is a sweet boy.

HECTOR: And these scenes are there in your eyes, down in the depths of them. Could I see them there?

HELEN: I don't know. Look.

HECTOR: Nothing. Nothing except the ashes of all those fires, the gold and the emerald in dust. How innocent it is, this crystal where the future is waiting. But there should be tears bathing it, and where are they? Would you cry, Helen, if you were going to be killed?

HELEN: I don't know. But I should scream. And I feel I shall scream if you go on at me like this, Hector. I am going to scream.

HECTOR: You will leave for Greece this evening, Helen, otherwise I shall kill you.

HELEN: But I want to leave! I'm prepared to leave. All that I'm trying to tell is that I simply can't manage to distinguish the ship that is going to carry me there. Nothing is shining in the least, neither the metal on the mast, nor the ring in

95

the captain's nose, nor the cabin-boy's eyes, nor anything.

HECTOR: You will go back on a grey sea under a grey sun. But we must have peace.

HELEN: I cannot see peace.

HECTOR: Ask Cassandra to make her appear for you. Cassandra is a sorceress. She can summon up shapes and spirits.

A MESSENGER (*entering*): Hector, Priam is asking for you. The priests are opposed to our shutting the Gates of War. They say the gods will consider it an insult.

HECTOR: It is curious how the gods can never speak for themselves in these difficult matters.

MESSENGER: They have spoken for themselves. A thunderbolt has fallen on the temple, several men have been killed, the entrails of the victims have been consulted, and they are unanimously against Helen's return to Greece.

HECTOR: I would give a good deal to be able to consult the entrails of the priests . . . I'll follow you. (*The Messenger goes.*) Well, now, Helen, do we agree about this?

HELEN: Yes.

HECTOR: From now on you will say what I tell you to say? You will do what I tell you to do?

HELEN: Yes.

HECTOR: When we come in front of Ulysses you won't contradict me, you will bear out everything I say?

HELEN: Yes.

HECTOR: Do you hear this, Cassandra? Listen to this solid wall of negation which says Yes! They have all given in to me. Paris has given in to me, Priam has given in to me, Helen has given in to me. And yet I can't help feeling that in each of these apparent victories I have been defeated. You set out thinking you are going to have to wrestle with giants; you brace yourself to conquer them, and you find yourself wrestling with something inflexible reflected in a woman's eye. You have said yes beautifully, Helen, and you're brimful of a stubborn determination to defy me!

HELEN: That's possible. But how can I help it? It isn't my own determination.

HECTOR: By what peculiar vagary did the world choose to place its mirror in this obtuse head?

HELEN: It's most regrettable, obviously. But can you see any way of defeating the obstinacy of a mirror?

HECTOR: Yes. I've been considering that for the past several minutes.

ANOTHER MESSENGER (*entering*): Hector, make haste. They are in a turmoil of revolt down on the beach. The Greek ships have been sighted, and they have hoisted their flag not masthead but hatchway. The honour of our navy is at stake. Priam is afraid the ambassador may be murdered as soon as he lands.

HECTOR: I leave you in charge of Helen, Cassandra. I must go and give my orders.

HELEN: If you break the mirror, will what is reflected in it cease to exist?

HECTOR: That is the whole question.

Exit Hector.

CASSANDRA: I never see anything at all, you know, either coloured or not. But I can feel the weight on me of every person who comes towards me. I know what is in store for them by the sensation of suffering which flows into my veins.

HELEN: Is it true that you are a sorceress? Could you really make Peace take shape and appear for us?

CASSANDRA: Peace? Very easily. She is always standing in her beggarly way on every threshold. Wait . . . you will see her now.

Peace appears.

HELEN: Oh, how pretty she is!

PEACE: Come to my rescue, Helen: help me!

HELEN: But how pale and wan she is.

PEACE: Pale and wan? What do you mean? Don't you see the gold shining in my hair?

HELEN: Gold? Well, perhaps a golden grey. It's very original.

PEACE: Golden grey? Is my gold now grey?

She disappears.

CASSANDRA: I think she means to make herself clearer.

Peace reappears, outrageously painted.

PEACE: Is that better now?
HELEN: I don't see her as well as I did before.
PEACE: Is that better?
CASSANDRA: Helen doesn't see you as well as she did.
PEACE: But you can see me: you are speaking to me.
CASSANDRA: It's my speciality to speak to the invisible.
PEACE: What is going on, then? Why are all the men in the city and along the beach making such a pandemonium?
CASSANDRA: Apparently their gods are insulted, and their honour is at stake.
PEACE: Their gods! Their honour!
CASSANDRA: Yes . . . You are ill!

Curtain

ACT TWO

A palace enclosure. At each corner a view of the sea. In the middle a monument, the Gates of War. They are wide open.

Helen and young Troilus.

HELEN: You, you, hey! You down there! Yes, it's you I'm calling. Come here.

TROILUS: No.

HELEN: What is your name?

TROILUS: Troilus.

HELEN: Come here.

TROILUS: No.

HELEN: Come here, Troilus! (*Troilus draws near.*) That's the way. You obey when you're called by your name: you are still very like a puppy. It's rather beguiling. Do you know you have made me call out to a man for the first time in my life. They keep so close to my side I have only usually to move my lips. I have called out to sea-gulls, to dogs, to the echoes, but never before to a man. You will pay for that. What's the matter? Are you trembling?

TROILUS: No, I'm not.

HELEN: You tremble, Troilus.

TROILUS: Yes, I do.

HELEN: Why are you always just behind me? If I walk with my back to the sun and suddenly stop, the head of your shadow stubs itself against my feet. That doesn't matter, as long as it doesn't overshoot them. Tell me what you want.

TROILUS: I don't want anything.

HELEN: Tell me what you want, Troilus!

TROILUS: Everything! I want everything!

HELEN: You want everything. The moon?

TROILUS: Everything! Everything and more!

HELEN: You're beginning to talk like a real man already; you want to kiss me!

TROILUS: No!

HELEN: You want to kiss me, isn't that it, Troilus?

TROILUS: I would kill myself directly afterwards!

HELEN: Come nearer. How old are you?

TROILUS: Fifteen. Alas!

HELEN: Bravo that alas. Have you kissed girls of your own age?

TROILUS: I hate them.

HELEN: But you have kissed them?

TROILUS: Well, yes, you're bound to kiss them, you kiss them all. I would give my life not to have kissed any of them.

HELEN: You seem prepared to get rid of quite a number of lives. Why haven't you said to me frankly: Helen, I want to kiss you! I don't see anything wrong in your kissing me. Kiss me.

TROILUS: Never.

HELEN: And then, when the day came to an end, you would have come quietly to where I was sitting on the battlements watching the sun go down over the islands, and you would have turned my head towards you with your hands – from golden it would have become dark, only shadow now, you would hardly have been able to see me – and you would have kissed me, and I should have been very happy. Why this is Troilus, I should have said to myself: young Troilus is kissing me! Kiss me.

TROILUS: Never.

HELEN: I see. You think, once you have kissed me, you would hate me?

TROILUS: Oh! Older men have all the luck, knowing how to say what they want to!

HELEN: You say it well enough.

Enter Paris.

PARIS: Take care, Helen, Troilus is a dangerous fellow.

HELEN: On the contrary. He wants to kiss me.

PARIS: Troilus, you know that if you kiss Helen, I shall kill you?

HELEN: Dying means nothing to him; no matter how often.

PARIS: What's the matter with him? Is he crouching to spring?
Is he going to take a leap at you? He's too nice a boy. Kiss
Helen, Troilus. I'll let you.

HELEN: If you can make up his mind to it you're cleverer than
I am.

*Troilus, who was about to hurl himself on Helen, immediately
draws back.*

PARIS: Listen, Troilus! Here's a committee of our revered
elders coming to shut the Gates of War. Kiss Helen in front
of them; it will make you famous. You want to be famous,
don't you, later on in life?

TROILUS: No. I want nobody to have heard of me.

PARIS: You don't want to be famous? You don't want to be
rich and powerful?

TROILUS: No. Poor. Ugly.

PARIS: Let me finish! So that you can have all the women you
want.

TROILUS: I don't want any, none at all, none.

PARIS: Here come the senators! Now you can choose: either
you kiss Helen in front of them, or I shall kiss her in front
of you. Would you rather I did it? All right! Look! . . .
Why, this was a new version of kiss you gave me, Helen.
What was it?

HELEN: The kiss I had ready for Troilus.

PARIS: You don't know what you're missing, my boy! Are you
leaving us? Good-bye, then.

HELEN: We shall kiss one another, Troilus. I'll answer for that.
(*Troilus goes.*) Troilus!

PARIS (*slightly unnerved*): You called very loudly, Helen.

Enter Demokos.

DEMOKOS: Helen, one moment! Look me full in the face. I've
got here in my hand a magnificent bird which I'm going to
set free. Are you looking? Here it is. Smooth back your hair,
and smile a beautiful smile.

PARIS: I don't see how the bird will fly any better if Helen smooths her hair and gives a beautiful smile.

HELEN: It can't do me any harm, anyway.

DEMOKOS: Don't move. One! Two! Three! There! It's all over, you can go now.

HELEN: Where was the bird?

DEMOKOS: It's a bird who knows how to make himself invisible.

HELEN: Ask him next time to tell you how he does it.

She goes.

PARIS: What is this nonsense?

DEMOKOS: I am writing a song on the subject of Helen's face. I needed to look at it closely, to engrave it, smiling, on my memory.

Enter Hecuba, Polyxene, Abneos, the Mathematician, and some Old Men.

HECUBA: Well, are you going to shut these Gates for us?

DEMOKOS: Certainly not. We might well have to open them again this very evening.

HECUBA: It is Hector's wish. And Hector will persuade Priam.

DEMOKOS: That is as we shall see. And what's more I have a surprise in store for Hector.

POLYXENE: Where do the Gates lead to, mama?

ABNEOS: To war, my child. When they are open it means there is war.

DEMOKOS: My friends . . .

HECUBA: War or not, it's an absurd symbolism, your Gateway, and those two great doors always left open look very unsightly. All the dogs stop there.

MATHEMATICIAN: This is no domestic matter. It concerns war and the gods.

HECUBA: Which is just as I said: the gods never remember to shut their doors.

POLYXENE: I remember to shut them very well, don't I, mama?

PARIS: And you even include your fingers in them, don't you, my pretty one?

DEMOKOS: May I ask for a moment of silence, Paris? Abneos, and you, Mathematician, and you, my friends: I asked you to meet here earlier than the time fixed for the ceremony so that we could hold our first council. And it promises well that this first council of war should be, not a council of generals, but a council of intellectuals. For it isn't enough in war-time to have our soldiers drilled, well-armed, and spectacular. It is absolutely necessary to bring their enthusiasm up to fever pitch. The physical intoxication which their officers will get from them by a generous allowance of cheap wine supplied at the right moment, will still be ineffective against the Greeks, unless it is reinforced by the spiritual and moral intoxication which the poets can pour into them. If we are too old to fight we can at least make sure that the fighting is savage. I see you have something to say on the subject, Abneos.

ABNEOS: Yes. We must make a war-song.

DEMOKOS: Very proper. A war requires a war-song.

PARIS: We have done without one up to now.

HECUBA: War itself sings quite loud enough.

ABNEOS: We have done without one because up to now we were fighting only barbarians. It was nothing more than a hunt, and the hunting horn was all we needed. But now with the Greeks we're entering a different region of war altogether.

DEMOKOS: Exactly so, Abneos. The Greeks don't fight with everybody.

PARIS: We already have a national anthem.

ABNEOS: Yes. But it's a song of peace.

PARIS: If you sing a song of peace with enough gestures and grimaces it becomes a war-song. What are the words we have already?

ABNEOS: You know them perfectly well. There's no spirit in them:

> "We cut and bind the harvest,
> We tread the vineyard's blood."

DEMOKOS: At the very most it's a war-song against farm produce. You won't frighten the Spartans by threatening a wheatfield.

PARIS: Sing it with a spear in your hand, and a dead body at your feet, you will be surprised.

HECUBA: It includes the word "blood", there's always that.

PARIS: The word "harvest" as well. War rather approves of the word "harvest".

ABNEOS: Why discuss it, when Demokos can invent an entirely new one in a couple of hours.

DEMOKOS: A couple of hours is rather short.

HECUBA: Don't be afraid; it's more than you need for it. And after the song will come the hymn, and after the hymn the cantata. As soon as war is declared it will be impossible to hold the poets back. Rhyme is still the most effective drum.

DEMOKOS: And the most useful, Hecuba: you don't know how wisely you speak. I know war. As long as war isn't with us, and the Gates are shut, each of us is free to insult it and execrate it as we will. But once war comes, its pride and autocracy is huge. You can gain its goodwill only by flattery and adoration. So the mission of those who understand how to speak and write is to compliment and praise war ceaselessly and indiscriminately, otherwise we shut ourselves out from his favour.

PARIS: Have you got an idea for your song already?

DEMOKOS: A marvellous idea, which no one will understand better than you. War must be tired of the mask we always give it, of Medusa's venomous hair and a Gorgon's lips. I have had the notion to compare War's face with Helen's. It will be enchanted by the comparison.

POLYXENE: What does War look like, mama?

HECUBA: Like your Aunt Helen.

POLYXENE: She is very pretty.

DEMOKOS: Then the discussion is closed. You can expect the war-song. Why are you looking worried, Mathematician?

MATHEMATICIAN: Because there are other things far more urgent than this war-song, far more urgent!

DEMOKOS: You think we should discuss the question of medals, false information, atrocity stories, and so on ?

MATHEMATICIAN: I think we should discuss the insulting epithets.

HECUBA: The insulting epithets ?

MATHEMATICIAN: Before they hurl their spears the Greek fighting-men hurl insults. You third cousin of a toad, they yell! You son of a sow! – They insult each other, like that! And they have a good reason for it. They know that the body is more vulnerable when self-respect has fled. Soldiers famous for their composure lose it immediately when they're treated as warts or maggots. We Trojans suffer from a grave shortage of insults.

DEMOKOS: The Mathematician is quite right. We are the only race in the world which doesn't insult its enemies before it kills them.

PARIS: You don't think it's enough that the civilians insult the enemy civilians ?

MATHEMATICIAN: The armies have to show the same hatred the civilians do. You know what dissemblers armies can be in this way. Leave them to themselves and they spend their time admiring each other. Their front lines very soon become the only ranks of real brotherhood in the world. So naturally, when the theatre of war is so full of mutual consideration, hatred is driven back on to the schools, the salons, the trades-people. If our soldiers aren't at least equal to the Greeks in the fury of their epithets, they will lose all taste for insults and calumny, and as a natural consequence all taste for war.

DEMOKOS: Suggestion adopted! We will organize a cursing parade this evening.

PARIS: I should have thought they're big enough to find their own curses.

DEMOKOS: What a mistake! Could you, adroit as you are, find your own effective curses ?

PARIS: I believe so.

DEMOKOS: You fool yourself. Come and stand face to face with Abneos and begin.

PARIS: Why Abneos?

DEMOKOS: Because he lends himself to this sort of thing, with his corpulence and one thing and another.

ABNEOS: Come on, then, speak up, you piece of pie-crust!

PARIS: No. Abneos doesn't inspire me. I'll start with you, if you don't mind.

DEMOKOS: With me? Certainly. You can let fly at ten paces. There we are. Begin.

HECUBA: Take a good look at him. You will be inspired.

PARIS: You old parasite! You filthy-footed iambic pentameter!

DEMOKOS: Just one second. To avoid any mistake you had better say who it is you're addressing.

PARIS: You're quite right! Demokos! Bloodshot bullock's eye! You fungus-ridden plum-tree!

DEMOKOS: Grammatically reasonable, but very naive. What is there in a fungus-ridden plum-tree to make me rise up foaming at the lips?

HECUBA: He also called you a bloodshot bullock's eye.

DEMOKOS: Bloodshot bullock's eye is better. But you see how you flounder, Paris? Search for something that can strike home to me. What are my faults, in your opinion?

PARIS: You are cowardly: your breath smells, and you have no talent.

DEMOKOS: You're asking for trouble!

PARIS: I was trying to please you.

POLYXENE: Why are we scolding Uncle Demokos, mama?

HECUBA: Because he is a cuckoo, dearest!

DEMOKOS: What did you say, Hecuba?

HECUBA: I was saying that you're a cuckoo, Demokos. If cuckoos had the absurdity, the affectation, the ugliness and the stench of vultures, you would be a cuckoo.

DEMOKOS: Wait a bit, Paris! Your mother is better at this than you are. Model yourselves on her. One hour's exercise each day for each soldier, and Hecuba has given us the superiority in insults which we badly need. As for the war-song, I'm not sure it wouldn't be wiser to entrust that to her as well.

HECUBA: If you like. But if so, I shouldn't say that war looks like Helen.

DEMOKOS: What would you say it looks like, in your opinion?

HECUBA: I will tell you when the Gates have been shut.

Enter Priam, Hector, Andromache, Busiris and presently Helen. During the closing of the Gates, Andromache takes little Polyxene aside and whispers a secret or an errand to her.

HECTOR: As they nearly are.

DEMOKOS: One moment, Hector!

HECTOR: Aren't we ready to begin the ceremony?

HECUBA: Surely? The hinges are swimming in oil.

HECTOR: Well, then.

PRIAM: What our friends want you to understand, Hector, is that war is ready, too. Consider carefully. They're not mistaken. If you shut these Gates, in a minute we may have to open them again.

HECUBA: Even one minute of peace is worth taking.

HECTOR: Father, you should know what peace means to men who have been fighting for months. It's like solid ground to someone who was drowning or sinking in the quicksands. Do let us get our feet on to a few inches of peace, touch it, if only with the tips of our toes.

PRIAM: Hector: consider: inflicting the word peace on the city today is as ruthless as though you gave it poison. You will take her off her guard, undermine her iron determination, debase, with the word peace, the accepted values of memory, affection, and hope. The soldiers will rush to buy the bread of peace, to drink the wine of peace, to hold in their arms the woman of peace, and in an hour you will put them back to face a war.

HECTOR: The war will never take place!

The sound of clamour near the Gates.

DEMOKOS: No? Listen!

HECTOR: Shut the Gates. This is where we shall meet the Greeks. Conversation will be bitter enough as it is. We must receive them in peace.

PRIAM: My son, are we even sure we should let the Greeks disembark?

HECTOR: Disembark they shall. This meeting with Ulysses is our last chance of peace.

DEMOKOS: Disembark they shall not. Our honour is at stake. We shall be the laughing-stock of the whole world.

HECTOR: And you're taking it upon yourself to recommend to the Senate an action which would certainly mean war?

DEMOKOS: Upon myself? No, not at all. Will you come forward now, Busiris? This is where your mission begins.

HECTOR: Who is this stranger?

DEMOKOS: He is the greatest living expert on the rights of nations. It's a lucky chance he should be passing through Troy today. You can't say that he's a biased witness. He is neutral. Our Senate is willing to abide by his decision, a decision which all other nations will agree with tomorrow.

HECTOR: And what is your opinion?

BUSIRIS: My opinion, Princes, based on my own observation and further inquiry, is that the Greeks, in relation to Troy, are guilty of three breaches of international law. If you give them permission to disembark you will have sacrificed your position as the aggrieved party, and so lost the universal sympathy which would certainly have been yours in the conflict to follow.

HECTOR: Explain yourself.

BUSIRIS: Firstly, they have hoisted their flag hatchway and not masthead. A ship of war, my dear Princes and colleagues, hoists its flag hatchway only when replying to a salute from a boat carrying cattle. Clearly, then, so to salute a city and a city's population is an insult. As it happens, we have a precedent. Last year the Greeks hoisted their flag hatchway when they were entering the port of Orphea. The reply was incisive. Orphea declared war.

HECTOR: And what happened?

BUSIRIS: Orphea was beaten. Orphea no longer exists, nor the Orpheans either.

HECUBA: Perfect.

BUSIRIS: But the annihilation of a people doesn't alter in the least their superior moral position.

HECTOR: Go on.

BUSIRIS: Secondly, on entering your territorial waters the Greeks adopted the formation known as frontal. At the last congress there was some talk of including this formation in the paragraph of measures called defensive-aggressive. I was very happy to be able to get it restored under its proper heading of aggressive-defensive: so without doubt it is now one of the subtle forms of naval manoeuvre which is a disguised form of blockade: that is to say, it constitutes a fault of the first degree! We have a precedent for this, as well. Five years ago the Greek navy adopted the frontal formation when they anchored outside Magnesia. Magnesia at once declared war.

HECTOR: Did they win it?

BUSIRIS: They lost it. There's not one stone of Magnesia still standing on another. But my redraft of the paragraph is still standing.

HECUBA: I congratulate you. We were beginning to be anxious.

HECTOR: Go on.

BUSIRIS: The third fault is not so serious. One of the Greek triremes has crept close in to shore without permission. Its captain, Ajax, the most unruly and impossible man among the Greeks, is climbing up towards the city, shouting scandal and provocation, and swearing he would like to kill Paris. But this is a very minor matter, from the international point of view, because it isn't, in any way, a formal breach of the law.

DEMOKOS: You have your information. The situation can only be resolved in one of two ways. To swallow an outrage, or return it. Choose.

HECTOR: Oneah, go and find Ajax. Head him off in this direction.

PARIS: I'm waiting here for him.

HECTOR: You will be good enough to stay in the Palace until I call for you. As for you, Busiris, you must understand that our city has no intention of being insulted by the Greeks.

BUSIRIS: I am not surprised. Troy's incorruptible pride is a legend all the world over.

HECTOR: You are going to provide me, here and now, with an argument which will allow our Senate to say that there has been no fault whatever on the part of our visitors, and with our pride untouched we welcome them here as our guests.

DEMOKOS: What nonsense is this?

BUSIRIS: It isn't in keeping with the facts, Hector.

HECTOR: My dear Busiris, all of us here know there's no better way of exercising the imagination than the study of law. No poet ever interpreted nature as freely as a lawyer interprets truth.

BUSIRIS: The Senate asked me for an opinion: I gave it.

HECTOR: And I ask you for an interpretation. An even subtler point of law.

BUSIRIS: It goes against my conscience.

HECTOR: Your conscience has seen Orphea destroyed, Magnesia destroyed: is it now contemplating, just as lightheartedly, the destruction of Troy?

HECUBA: Yes. He comes from Syracuse.

HECTOR: I do beg of you, Busiris. The lives of two countries depend on this. Help us.

BUSIRIS: Truth is the only help I can give you.

HECTOR: Precisely. Discover a truth which saves us. What is the use of justice if it doesn't hammer out a shield for innocent people? Forge us a truth. If you can't, there is one thing I can tell you, quite simply: we shall hold you here for as long as the war goes on.

BUSIRIS: What are you saying?

DEMOKOS: You're abusing your position, Hector!

HECUBA: During war we imprison the rights of man. There seems no reason why we shouldn't imprison a lawyer.

HECTOR: I mean what I say, Busiris. I've never failed yet to keep my promises, or my threats. And now either these guards are going to take you off to prison for a year or two, or else you leave here, this evening, heaped with gold. With this in mind, you can dispassionately examine the evidence once again.

BUSIRIS: Actually there are certain mitigating arguments.

HECTOR: I was sure there were.

BUSIRIS: In the case of the first fault, for instance, when the cattle-boat salute is given in certain seas where the shores are fertile, it could be interpreted as a salute from the sailors to the farmers.

HECTOR: That would be, in fact, the logical interpretation. The salute of the sea to the earth.

BUSIRIS: Not to mention that the cargo of cattle might easily be a cargo of bulls. In that case the homage would verge on flattery.

HECTOR: There you are. You've understood what I meant. We've arrived at our point of view.

BUSIRIS: And as to the frontal formation, that could as easily mean a promise as a provocation. Women wanting children give themselves not from the side but face to face.

HECTOR: Decisive argument.

BUSIRIS: Then, again, the Greek ships have huge carved nymphs for figureheads. A woman who comes towards you naked and open-armed is not a threat but an offer. An offer to talk, at any rate.

HECTOR: So there we have our honour safe and sound, Demokos. The next step is to make this consultation with Busiris public. Meanwhile, Minos, tell the port authorities to let Ulysses disembark without any loss of time.

DEMOKOS: It's no use even trying to discuss honour with these fighting men. They trade on the fact that you can't treat them as cowards.

MATHEMATICIAN: At any rate, Hector, deliver the Oration for the Dead. That will make you think again.

HECTOR: There's not going to be an Oration for the Dead.

PRIAM: But it's a part of the ceremony. The victorious general must always speak in honour of the dead when the Gates are closed.

HECTOR: An Oration for the Dead of a war is a hypocritical

speech in defence of the living, a plea for acquittal. I am not so sure of my innocence.

DEMOKOS: The High Command is not responsible.

HECTOR: Alas, no one is: nor the Gods either. Besides, I have given my oration for the dead already. I gave it to them in their last minute of life, when they were lying on the battle-field, on a little slope of olive-trees, while they could still attend me with what was left of their sight and hearing. I can tell you what I said to them. There was one, disembowelled, already turning up the whites of his eyes, and I said to him: 'It's not so bad, you know, it's not so bad; you will do all right, old man'. And one with his skull split in two; I said: 'You look pretty comical with that broken nose'. And my little equerry, with his left arm hanging useless and his last blood flowing out of him; and I said: 'It's a good thing for you it's the left arm you've splintered'. I am happy I gave them one final swig of life; it was all they asked for; they died drinking it. And there's nothing else to be said. Shut the Gates.

POLYXENE: Did the little equerry die, as well?

HECTOR: Yes, puss-cat. He died. He stretched out his right arm. Someone I couldn't see took him by his perfect hand. And then he died.

DEMOKOS: Our general seems to confuse remarks made to the dying with the Oration for the Dead.

PRIAM: Why must you be so stubborn, Hector?

HECTOR: Very well: you shall have the Oration. (*He takes a position below the gates.*) – You who cannot hear us, who cannot see us, listen to these words, look at those who come to honour you. We have won the war. I know that's of no moment to you. You are the victors, too. But we are victori-ous, and still live. That's where the difference is between us and why I'm ashamed. I don't know whether, among the crowd of the dead, any privilege is given to men who died victorious. But the living, whether victorious or not, have privilege enough. We have our eyes. We see the sun. We do what all men do under the sun. We eat. We drink. By the moon, we sleep with our wives. And with yours, now you have gone.

DEMOKOS: You insult the dead!

HECTOR: Do you think so?

DEMOKOS: Either the dead or the living.

HECTOR: There is a distinction.

PRIAM: Come to the peroration, Hector. The Greeks are coming ashore.

HECTOR: I will come to it now . . . Breathe in this incense, touch these offerings, you who can neither smell nor touch. And understand, since I speak to you sincerely, I haven't an equal tenderness and respect for all of you. Though all of you are the dead, with you as with us who survive there are men of courage and men of fear, and you can't make me confuse, for the sake of a ceremony, the dead I admire with those I can't admire. But what I have to say to you today is that war seems to me the most sordid, hypocritical way of making all men equal: and I accept death neither as a punishment or expiation for the coward, nor as a reward to the living. So, whatever you may be, absent, forgotten, purposeless, unresting, without existence, one thing is certain when we close these Gates: we must ask you to forgive us, we, the deserters who survive you, who feel we have stolen two great privileges. I hope the sound of their names will never reach you: the warmth of the living body, and the sky.

POLYXENE: The Gates are shutting, mama!

HECUBA: Yes, darling.

POLYXENE: The dead men are pushing them shut.

HECUBA: They help, a little.

POLYXENE: They're helping quite a lot, especially over on the right.

HECTOR: Is it done? Are they shut?

GUARD: Tight as a clam.

HECTOR: We're at peace, father, we're at peace.

HECUBA: We're at peace!

POLYXENE: It feels much better, doesn't it, mama?

HECTOR: Indeed it does.

POLYXENE: I feel much better, anyway.

The sound of the Greeks' music.

A MESSENGER: The Greeks have landed, Priam!

DEMOKOS: What music! What frightful music! It's the most anti-Trojan music there could possibly be! Let's go and give them a welcome to match it.

HECTOR: Receive them royally, bring them here safely. You are responsible.

MATHEMATICIAN: At any rate we ought to counter with some Trojan music. Hector, if we can't be indignant any other way, you can authorize a battle of music.

CROWD: The Greeks! The Greeks!

MESSENGER: Ulysses is on the landing-stage, Priam. Where are we to take him?

PRIAM: Conduct him here. Send word to us in the palace when he comes. Keep with us, Paris. We don't want you too much in evidence just yet.

HECTOR: Let's go and prepare what we shall say to the Greeks, father.

DEMOKOS: You'd better prepare it somewhat better than your speech for the dead; you're likely to meet more contradiction. (*Exeunt Priam and his sons.*) If you are going with them, tell us before you go, Hecuba, what it is you think war looks like.

HECUBA: You insist on knowing?

DEMOKOS: If you've seen what it looks like, tell us.

HECUBA: Like the bottom of a baboon. When the baboon is up in a tree, with its hind end facing us, there is the face of war exactly: scarlet, scaly, glazed, framed in a clotted, filthy wig.

DEMOKOS: So he has two faces: this you describe, and Helen's.

Exit.

ANDROMACHE: Here is Helen now. Polyxene, you remember what you have to say to her?

POLYXENE: Yes.

114

ANDROMACHE: Go to her, then.

Enter Helen.

HELEN: Do you want to talk to me, darling?

POLYXENE: Yes, Aunt Helen.

HELEN: It must be important, you're so very tense.

POLYXENE: Yes, Aunt Helen.

HELEN: Is it something you can't tell me without standing so stiffly?

POLYXENE: No, Aunt Helen.

HELEN: Do tell me, then; you make me feel terrible when you stand there like a little stick.

POLYXENE: Aunt Helen, if you love anyone, please go away.

HELEN: Why should I go away, darling?

POLYXENE: Because of the war.

HELEN: Do you know about war already, then?

POLYXENE: I don't exactly know about it. I think it means we have to die.

HELEN: And do you know what dying is?

POLYXENE: I don't exactly. I think it means we don't feel anything any more.

HELEN: What exactly was it that Andromache told you to ask me?

POLYXENE: If you love us at all, please to go away.

HELEN: That doesn't seem to me very logical. If you loved someone you wouldn't leave them?

POLYXENE: Oh, no! Never!

HELEN: Which would you rather do: go right away from Hecuba, or never feel anything any more?

POLYXENE: Oh, never feel anything! I would rather stay, and never feel anything any more.

HELEN: You see how badly you put things to me. If I'm to leave you, I mustn't love you. Would you rather I didn't love you?

POLYXENE: Oh, no! I want you to love me.

HELEN: In other words, you didn't know what you were saying, did you?

POLYXENE: No.

HECUBA (*offstage*): Polyxene!

Enter Hecuba.

Are you deaf, Polyxene? Why did you shut your eyes when you saw me? Are you playing at being a statue? Come with me.

HELEN: She is teaching herself not to feel anything. But she has no gift for it.

HECUBA: Can you hear me, Polyxene? And see me?

POLYXENE: Yes, I can hear you. I can see you, too.

HECUBA: Why are you crying? Don't you like to see and hear me?

POLYXENE: If I do, you will go away.

HECUBA: I think it would be better, Helen, if you left Polyxene alone. She is too sensitive to touch the insensitive, even through your beautiful dress and your beautiful voice.

HELEN: I quite agree with you. I advise Andromache to carry her own messages. Kiss me, Polyxene. I shall go away this evening, since that is what you would like.

POLYXENE: Don't go! Don't go!

HELEN: Bravo! You are quite loosened up again!

HECUBA: Are you coming with us, Andromache?

ANDROMACHE: No: I shall wait here.

Exeunt Hecuba and Polyxene.

HELEN: You want an explanation?

ANDROMACHE: I believe it's necessary.

HELEN: Listen to the way they're shouting and arguing down below. Isn't that enough? Do you and I have to have explanations, too? And what explanations, since I'm leaving here anyway?

ANDROMACHE: Whether you go or stay isn't any longer the problem.

HELEN: Tell Hector that. You will make his day easier.

ANDROMACHE: Yes, Hector is obsessed by the thought of getting you away. All men are the same. They take no notice

116

of the stag in the thicket because they're already chasing the hare. Perhaps men can hunt like that. But not the gods.

HELEN: If you have discovered what the gods are after in this affair, I congratulate you.

ANDROMACHE: I don't know that the gods are after anything. But there is something the universe is after. Ever since this morning, it seems to me, everything has begged and cried out for it, men, animals, even the leaves on the trees and my own child, not yet born.

HELEN: Cried out for what?

ANDROMACHE: That you should love Paris.

HELEN: If they know so certainly that I don't love Paris, they are better informed than I am.

ANDROMACHE: But you don't love him! You could love him, perhaps. But, at present, you are both living in a misunderstanding.

HELEN: I live with him happily, amicably, in complete agreement. We understand each other so well, I don't really see how this can be called a misunderstanding.

ANDROMACHE: Agreement is never reached in love. The life of a wife and husband who love each other is never at rest. Whether the marriage is true or false, the marriage portion is the same: elemental discord. Hector is my absolute opposite. He shares none of my tastes. We pass our days either getting the better of one another, or sacrificing ourselves. There is no tranquillity for lovers.

HELEN: And if I went pale whenever I saw Paris: and my eyes filled with tears, and the palms of my hands were moist, you think Menelaus would be delighted, and the Greeks pleased and quite satisfied?

ANDROMACHE: It wouldn't much matter then what the Greeks thought.

HELEN: And the war would never happen?

ANDROMACHE: Perhaps, indeed, it would never happen. Perhaps if you loved him, love would call to the rescue one of its own equals: generosity or intelligence. No one, not even destiny itself, attacks devotion lightheartedly.

And even if the war did happen, why, I think even then –

HELEN: Then it wouldn't be the same war, I suppose.

ANDROMACHE: Oh, no, Helen! You know what this struggle is going to be. Fate would never take so many precautions for an ordinary quarrel. It means to build the future on this war, the future of our countries and our peoples, and our ways of thinking. It won't be so bad if our thoughts and our future are built on the story of a man and a woman who truly love each other. But fate hasn't noticed yet that you are lovers only on paper, officially. To think that we're going to suffer and die only for a pair of theoretical lovers: and the splendour and calamity of the age to come will be founded on a trivial adventure between two people who don't love each other – that's what is so horrible.

HELEN: If everybody thinks that we love each other, it comes to the same thing.

ANDROMACHE: They don't think so. But no one will admit that he doesn't. Everyone, when there's war in the air, learns to live in a new element: falsehood. Everybody lies. Our old men don't worship beauty: they worship themselves, they worship ugliness. And this indignation the Greeks are showing us is a lie. God knows, they're amused enough at what you can do with Paris! Their boats, in the bay, with their patriotic anthems and their streamers flying, are a falsehood of the sea. And Hector's life and my son's life, too, are going to be played out in hypocrisy and pretence.

HELEN: So?

ANDROMACHE: I beg of you, Helen. You see how I'm pressed against you as though I were begging you to love me. Love Paris! Or tell me that I'm mistaken! Tell me that you would kill yourself if Paris were to die! Tell me that you would even let yourself be disfigured if it would keep him alive. Then the war will only be a scourge, not an injustice.

HELEN: You are being very difficult. I don't think my way of loving is as bad as all that. Certainly I don't get upset and ill when Paris leaves me to play bowls or go fishing for eels. But I do feel commanded by him, magnetically attracted.

Magnetism is a kind of love, as much as devotion. And it's an old and fruitful passion in its own way, as desperate devotion and passionate weeping are in theirs. I'm as content in this love as a star in a constellation. It's my own centre of gravity; I shine there; it's the way I breathe, and the way I take life in my arms. And it's easy to see what sons this love can produce: tall, clear-cut boys, of great distinction, with fine fingers and short noses. What will it all become if I fill it with jealousy, with emotion, and anxiety? The world is nervous enough already: look at yourself!

ANDROMACHE: Fill it with pity, Helen. That's the only help the world needs.

HELEN: There we are; I knew it would come; the word has been said.

ANDROMACHE: What word?

HELEN: The word "pity". You must talk to someone else. I'm afraid I'm not very good at pity.

ANDROMACHE: Because you don't know unhappiness.

HELEN: Maybe. It could also be that I think of unhappy people as my equals, I accept them, and I don't think of my health and my position and beauty as any better than their misery. It's a sense of brotherhood I have.

ANDROMACHE: You're blaspheming, Helen.

HELEN: I am sure people pity others to the same extent that they would pity themselves. Unhappiness and ugliness are mirrors they can't bear to look into. I haven't any pity for myself. You will see, if war breaks out. I'll put up with hunger and pain better than you will. And insults, too. Do you think I don't hear what the Trojan women say when I'm going past them? They treat me like a slut. They say that the morning light shows me up for what they think me. It may be true, or it may not be. It doesn't matter to me, one way or the other.

ANDROMACHE: Stop, Helen!

HELEN: And of course I can see, in what your husband called the coloured picture-book in my head, pictures of Helen grown old, flabby, toothless, sitting hunched-up in the kitchen, sucking sweets. I can see the white enamel I've plastered over my wrinkles, and the bright colours the sweets are, very clearly. But it leaves me completely indifferent.

ANDROMACHE: I am lost.

HELEN: Why? If you're content with one perfect couple to make the war acceptable, there is always you and Hector, Andromache.

Enter Ajax, then Hector.

AJAX: Where is he? Where's he hiding himself? A coward! A typical Trojan!

HECTOR: Who are you looking for?

AJAX: I'm looking for Paris.

HECTOR: I am his brother.

AJAX: Beautiful family! I am Ajax! What's your name?

HECTOR: My name's Hector.

AJAX: It ought to be pimp!

HECTOR: I see that Greece has sent over her diplomats. What do you want?

AJAX: War.

HECTOR: Not a hope. Why do you want it?

AJAX: Your brother carried off Helen.

HECTOR: I am told she was willing.

AJAX: A Greek woman can do what she likes. She doesn't have to ask permission from you. He carried her off. It's a reason for war.

HECTOR: We can offer our apologies.

AJAX: What's a Trojan's apology? We're not leaving here without your declaration of war.

HECTOR: Declare it yourselves.

AJAX: All right, we will. As from this evening.

HECTOR: That's a lie. You won't declare war. There isn't an island in the archipelago that will back you if we aren't in any way responsible. And we don't intend to be.

AJAX: Will you declare it yourself, personally, if I call you a coward?

HECTOR: That is a name I accept.

AJAX: I've never known such unmilitary reaction! Suppose I tell you what the people of Greece thinks of Troy, that Troy is a cess-pit of vice and stupidity?

HECTOR: Troy is obstinate. You won't get your war.

AJAX: Suppose I spit on her?

HECTOR: Spit.

AJAX: Suppose I strike you, you, one of her princes?

HECTOR: Try it.

AJAX: Suppose I slap your face, you disgusting example of Troy's conceit and her spurious honour?

HECTOR: Strike.

AJAX (*striking him*): There. If this lady's your wife she must be proud of you.

HECTOR: I know her. She is proud.

Enter Demokos.

DEMOKOS: What's all the noise about? What does this drunkard want, Hector?

HECTOR: He has got what he wants.

DEMOKOS: What is going on, Andromache?

ANDROMACHE: Nothing.

AJAX: Two times nothing. A Greek hits Hector, and Hector puts up with it.

DEMOKOS: Is this true, Hector?

HECTOR: Completely false, isn't it, Helen?

HELEN: The Greeks are great liars. Greek men, I mean.

AJAX: Is it natural for him to have one cheek redder than the other?

HECTOR: Yes. I am healthier on that side.

DEMOKOS: Tell the truth, Hector. Has he dared to raise his hand against you?

HECTOR: That is my concern.

DEMOKOS: It's the concern of war. You are the figurehead of Troy.

HECTOR: Exactly. No one is going to slap a figurehead.

DEMOKOS: Who are you, you brute? I am Demokos, second son of Achichaos!

AJAX: The second son of Achichaos? How do you do? Tell me: is it as serious to slap a second son of Achichaos as to strike Hector?

DEMOKOS: Quite as serious, you drunk. I am the head of the Senate. If you want war, war to the death, you have only to try.

AJAX: All right. I'll try. (*He slaps Demokos.*)

DEMOKOS: Trojans! Soldiers! To the rescue!

HECTOR: Be quiet, Demokos!

DEMOKOS: To arms! Troy's been insulted! Vengeance!

HECTOR: Be quiet, I tell you.

DEMOKOS: I *will* shout! I'll rouse the city!

HECTOR: Be quiet! If you won't, I shall hit you, too!

DEMOKOS: Priam, Anchises! Come and see the shame of Troy burning on Hector's face!

Hector strikes Demokos. Ajax laughs. During the scene, Priam and his lords group themselves ready to receive Ulysses.

PRIAM: What are you shouting for, Demokos?

DEMOKOS: I have been struck.

AJAX: Go and complain to Achichaos!

PRIAM: Who struck you?

DEMOKOS: Hector! Ajax! Ajax! Hector!

PARIS: What is he talking about? He's mad!

HECTOR: Nobody struck him, did they, Helen?

HELEN: I was watching most carefully, and I didn't notice anything.

AJAX: Both his cheeks are the same colour.

PARIS: Poets often get upset for no reason. It's what they call their inspiration. We shall get a new national anthem out of it.

DEMOKOS: You will pay for this, Hector.

VOICES: Ulysses! Here is Ulysses!

Ajax goes amicably to Hector.

AJAX: Well done. Plenty of pluck. Noble adversary. A beautiful hit.

HECTOR : I did my best.

AJAX : Excellent method, too. Straight elbow. The wrist on an angle. Safe position for the carpus and metacarpus. Your slap must be stronger than mine is.

HECTOR : I doubt it.

AJAX : You must be able to throw a javelin magnificently with this iron forearm and this shoulder-bone for a pivot.

HECTOR : Eighty yards.

AJAX : My deepest respect! My dear Hector, forgive me. I withdraw my threats, I take back my slap. We have enemies in common, in the sons of Achichaos. I won't fight with anybody who shares with me an enmity for the sons of Achichaos. Not another mention of war. I don't know what Ulysses has got in mind, but count on me to arrange the whole thing.

He goes towards Ulysses and comes back with him.

ANDROMACHE : I love you, Hector.

HECTOR (*showing his cheek*): Yes; but don't kiss me just yet.

ANDROMACHE : You have won this round, as well. Be confident.

HECTOR : I win every round. But still with each victory the prize escapes me.

ULYSSES : Priam and Hector ?

PRIAM : Yes. And behind us, Troy, and the suburbs of Troy, and the land of Troy, and the Hellespont.

ULYSSES : I am Ulysses.

PRIAM : This is Anchises.

ULYSSES : There are many people here for a diplomatic conversation.

PRIAM : And here is Helen.

ULYSSES : Good morning, my queen.

HELEN : I've grown younger here, Ulysses. I've become a princess again.

PRIAM : We are ready to listen to you.

AJAX : Ulysses, you speak to Priam. I will speak to Hector.

ULYSSES : Priam, we have come to take Helen home again.

AJAX: You do understand, don't you, Hector? We can't have things happening like this.

ULYSSES: Greece and Menelaus cry out for vengeance.

AJAX: If deceived husbands can't cry out for vengeance, what can they do?

ULYSSES: Deliver Helen over to us within an hour. Otherwise it means war.

HECTOR: But if we give Helen back to you give us your assurance there will be peace.

AJAX: Utter tranquillity.

HECTOR: If she goes on board within an hour, the matter is closed.

AJAX: And all is forgotten.

HECTOR: I think there's no doubt we can come to an understanding, can we not, Helen?

HELEN: Yes, no doubt.

ULYSSES: You don't mean to say that Helen is being given back to us?

HECTOR: Exactly that. She is ready.

AJAX: What about her baggage? She is sure to have more to take back than when she came.

HECTOR: We return her to you, bag and baggage, and you guarantee peace. No reprisals, no vengeance!

AJAX: A woman is lost, a woman is found, and we're back where we were. Perfect! Isn't it, Ulysses?

ULYSSES: Just wait a moment. I guarantee nothing. Before we say there are going to be no reprisals we have to be sure there has been no cause for reprisals. We have to make sure that Menelaus will find Helen exactly as she was when she was taken from him.

HECTOR: How is he going to discover any difference?

ULYSSES: A husband is very perceptive when a world-wide scandal has put him on his guard. Paris will have had to have respected Helen. And if that isn't so . . .

CROWD: Oh, no! It isn't so!

ONE VOICE: Not exactly!

HECTOR: And if it is so?

ULYSSES : Where is this leading us, Hector ?

HECTOR : Paris has not touched Helen. They have both taken me into their confidence.

ULYSSES : What is this absurd story ?

HECTOR : The true story, isn't it, Helen ?

HELEN : Why does it seem to you so extraordinary ?

A VOICE : It's terrible! It puts us to shame!

HECTOR : Why do you have to smile, Ulysses ? Do you see the slightest indication in Helen that she has failed in her duty ?

ULYSSES : I'm not looking for one. Water leaves less mark on a duck's back than dishonour does on a woman.

PARIS : You're speaking to a queen.

ULYSSES : Present queens excepted, naturally. So, Paris, you have carried off this queen, carried her off naked; and I imagine that you didn't go into the water wearing all your armour; and yet you weren't seized by any taste or desire for her ?

PARIS : A naked queen is dressed in her dignity.

HELEN : She has only to remember to keep it on.

ULYSSES. How long did the voyage last ? I took three days with my ships, which are faster than yours.

VOICES : What are these intolerable insults to the Trojan navy ?

A VOICE : Your winds are faster! Not your ships!

ULYSSES : Let us say three days, if you like. Where was the queen during those three days ?

PARIS : Lying down on the deck.

ULYSSES : And Paris was where ? In the crow's nest ?

HELEN : Lying beside me.

ULYSSES : Was he reading as he lay beside you ? Or fishing for goldfish ?

HELEN : Sometimes he fanned me.

ULYSSES : Without ever touching you ?

HELEN : One day, the second day, I think it was, he kissed my hand.

ULYSSES : Your hand! I see. An outbreak of the animal in him.

HELEN : I thought it was more dignified to take no notice.

ULYSSES : The rolling of the ship didn't throw you towards

each other? I don't think it's an insult to the Trojan navy
to suggest that its ships roll?

A VOICE: They roll much less than the Greek ships pitch!

AJAX: Pitch? Our Greek ships? If they seem to be pitching it's
because of their high prows and their scooped-out sterns!

A VOICE: Oh, yes! The arrogant face and the flat behind, that's
Greek all right.

ULYSSES: And what about the three nights you were sailing?
The stars appeared and vanished again three times over the
pair of you. Do you remember nothing of those three nights?

HELEN: I don't know. Oh, yes! I'd forgotten. I learnt a lot
more about the stars.

ULYSSES: While you were asleep, perhaps, he might have
taken you . . .

HELEN: A mosquito can wake me.

HECTOR: They will both swear to you, if you like, by your
goddess Aphrodite.

ULYSSES: We can do without that. I know what Aphrodite is.
Her favourite oath is a perjury. – It's a curious story you're
telling me: and it will certainly destroy the idea that the rest
of the Archipelago has always had of the Trojans.

PARIS: Why, what do they think of us in the Archipelago?

ULYSSES: You're thought of as less accomplished at trading
than we are, but handsome and irresistible. Go on with your
story, Paris. It's an interesting contribution to the study of
human behaviour. What good reason could you have possibly
had for respecting Helen when you had her at your
mercy?

PARIS: I . . . I loved her.

HELEN: If you don't know what love is, Ulysses, I shouldn't
venture on the subject.

ULYSSES: You must admit, Helen, you would never have
followed him if you had known the Trojans were impotent.

VOICES: Shame! Muzzle him! Bring your women here, and
you'll soon see! And your grandmother!

ULYSSES: I expressed myself badly. I meant that Paris, the
handsome Paris, is impotent.

A VOICE: Why don't you say something, Paris? Are you going to make us the laughing-stock of the world?

PARIS: Hector, you can see, this is a most unpleasant situation for me!

HECTOR: You have to put up with it only a few minutes longer. Good-bye, Helen. And I hope your virtue will become as proverbial as your frailty might have done.

HELEN: That doesn't worry me. The centuries always give us the recognition we deserve.

ULYSSES: Paris the impotent, that's a very good surname! If you care to, Helen, you can kiss him for once.

PARIS: Hector!

FIRST TOPMAN: Are you going to tolerate this farce, commander?

HECTOR: Be quiet! I am in charge here!

TOPMAN: And a rotten job you make of it! We've stood quite enough. We'll tell you, we, Paris's own seamen, we'll tell you what he did with your queen!

VOICES: Bravo! Tell him!

TOPMAN: He's sacrificing himself on his brother's orders. I was an officer on board his ship. I saw everything.

HECTOR: You were quite wrong.

TOPMAN: Do you think a Trojan sailor doesn't know what he sees? I can tell the sex of a seagull thirty yards off. Come over here, Olpides. Olpides was up in the crow's nest. He saw everything from on top. I was standing on the stairs in the hatchway. My head was exactly on a level with them, like a cat on the end of a bed. Shall I tell him, Trojans?

HECTOR: Silence!

VOICES: Tell him! Go on and tell him!

TOPMAN: And they hadn't been on board more than two minutes, wasn't that true, Olpides?

OLPIDES: Only time enough for the queen to dry herself, being just come up out of the water, and to comb the parting into her hair again. I could see her parting, from her forehead over to the nape of her neck, from where I was.

TOPMAN: And he sent us all down into the hold, except the two of us whom he couldn't see.

OLPIDES: And without a pilot, the ship drifted due north. There was no wind, and yet the sails were bellied out full.

TOPMAN: And when I looked out from where I was hiding, what I should have seen was the outline of one body, but what I did see was in the shape of two, like a wheaten loaf and rye bread, baking in the oven together.

OLPIDES: But from up where I was, I more often saw one body than two, but sometimes it was white, and sometimes it was golden brown.

TOPMAN: So much for impotence! And as for respectful, inexpressive love, and unspoken affection, you tell him, Olpides, what you heard from your ledge up there! Women's voices carry upwards, men's voices stay on the ground. I shall tell you what Paris said.

OLPIDES: She called him her ladybird, her little ewe-lamb.

TOPMAN: And he called her his lion, his panther. They reversed sexes. Because they were being so affectionate. It's not unusual.

OLPIDES: And then she said: "You are my darling oak-tree, I put my arms round you as if you were an oak-tree". When you're at sea you think about trees, I suppose.

TOPMAN: And he called her his birch-tree: "My trembling silver birch-tree!" I remember the word birch-tree very well. It's a Russian tree.

OLPIDES: And I had to stay up in the crow's nest all night. You don't half get thirsty up there, and hungry, and everything else.

TOPMAN: And when at last they got up from the deck to go to bed they swayed on their feet. And that's how your wife Penelope would have got on with Trojan impotence.

VOICES: Bravo! Bravo!

A WOMAN'S VOICE: All praise to Paris.

A JOVIAL MAN: Render to Paris what belongs to Paris!

HECTOR: This is a pack of lies, isn't it, Helen?

ULYSSES: Helen is listening enraptured.

HELEN: I forgot they were talking about me. They sound so wonderfully convincing.

ULYSSES: Do you dare to say they are lying, Paris?

PARIS: In some of the particulars, yes, I think they are.

TOPMAN: We're not lying, either in the general or the particular. Are we, Olpides? Do you deny the expressions of love you used? Do you deny the word panther?

PARIS: Not especially the word panther.

TOPMAN: Well, birch-tree, then? I see. It's the phrase "trembling silver birch-tree" that embarrasses you. Well, like it or not, you used it. I swear you used it, and anyway what is there to blush about in the word "birch-tree"? I have seen these silver birch-trees trembling against the snow in winter-time, by the shores of the Caspian, with their rings of black bark apparently separated by rings of space, so that you wondered what was carrying the branches. And I've seen them at the height of summer, beside the canal at Astrakhan, with their white rings like fresh mushrooms. And the leaves talked and made signs to me. To see them quivering, gold above and silver underneath, it makes your heart melt! I could have wept like a woman, isn't that true, Olpides? That's how I feel about the birch-tree.

CROWD: Bravo! Bravo!

ANOTHER SAILOR: And it wasn't only the topman and Olpides who saw them, Priam. The entire crew came wriggling up through the hatches and peering under the handrails. The whole ship was one great spy-glass.

THIRD SAILOR: Spying out love.

ULYSSES: There you have it, Hector!

HECTOR: Be quiet, the lot of you.

TOPMAN: Well, keep this quiet, if you can!

Iris appears in the sky.

PEOPLE: Iris! Iris!

PARIS: Has Aphrodite sent you?

IRIS: Yes, Aphrodite sent me, and told me that I should say

to you that love is the world's chief law. Whatever strengthens love becomes in itself sacred, even falsehood, avarice, or luxury. She takes all lovers under her protection, from the king to the goat-herd. And she forbids both of you, Hector and Ulysses, to separate Paris from Helen. Or else there will be war.

PARIS AND THE OLD MEN: Thank you, Iris.

HECTOR: Is there any message from Pallas Athene?

IRIS: Yes; Pallas Athene told me that I should say to you that reason is the chief law of the world. All who are lovers, she wishes me to say, are out of their minds. She would like you to tell her quite frankly what is more ridiculous than the mating of cocks with hens or flies with flies. And she orders both of you, Hector, and Ulysses, to separate Helen from this Paris of the curly hair. Or else there will be war.

HECTOR AND THE WOMEN: Thank you, Iris!

PRIAM: Oh, my son, it isn't Aphrodite nor Pallas Athene who rules the world. What is it Zeus commands us to do in this time of uncertainty?

IRIS: Zeus, the master of the gods, told me that I should say to you that those who see in the world nothing but love are as foolish as those who cannot see it at all. It is wise, Zeus, master of the gods informs you, it is wise sometimes to make love, and at other times not to make love. The decision he gives to Hector and Ulysses, is to separate Helen and Paris without separating them. He orders all the rest of you to go away and leave the negotiators to face each other. And let them so arrange matters that there will be no war. Or else – he swears to you: he swears there will be war.

Exit Iris.

HECTOR: At your service, Ulysses!

ULYSSES: At your service.

All withdraw. A great rainbow is seen in the sky .

HELEN: How very like Iris to leave her scarf behind.

HECTOR: Now we come to the real tussle, Ulysses.

ULYSSES: Yes: out of which either war or peace is going to come.

HECTOR: Will war come of it?

ULYSSES: We shall know in five minutes' time.

HECTOR: If it's to be a battle of words, my chances are small.

ULYSSES: I believe it will be more a battle of weight. It's as though we were one on each side of a pair of scales. How we weigh in the balance will be what counts in the end.

HECTOR: How we weigh in the balance? And what is my weight, Ulysses? My weight is a young man, a young woman, an unborn child. Joy of life, belief in life, a response to whatever's natural and good.

ULYSSES: And my weight is the mature man, the wife thirty-five years old, the son whose height I measure each month with notches against the doorpost of the palace. My weight is the pleasure of living, and a mistrust of life.

HECTOR: Hunting, courage, loyalty, love.

ULYSSES: Circumspection in the presence of the gods, of men, and everything else.

HECTOR: The Phrygian oak-tree, all the leafy, thick-set oak-trees that grow on our hills with our curly-coated oxen.

ULYSSES: The power and wisdom of the olive-tree.

HECTOR: I weigh the hawk, I look straight into the sun.

ULYSSES: I weigh the owl.

HECTOR: I weigh the whole race of humble peasants, hard-working craftsmen, thousands of ploughs and looms, forges and anvils . . . Why is it, when I put all these in the scale in front of you, all at once they seem to me to weigh so light?

ULYSSES: I am the weight of this incorruptible, unpitying air of these coasts and islands.

HECTOR: Why go on? The scales have tipped.

ULYSSES: To my side? Yes, I think so.

HECTOR: And you want war?

ULYSSES: I don't want it. But I'm less sure whether war may not want us.

HECTOR: Our peoples have brought us together to prevent it. Our meeting itself shows that there is still some hope.

ULYSSES: You are young, Hector! It's usual on the eve of every war, for the two leaders of the peoples concerned to meet privately at some innocent village, on a terrace in a garden overlooking a lake. And they decide together that war is the world's worst scourge, and as they watch the rippling reflexions in the water, with magnolia petals dropping on to their shoulders, they are both of them peace-loving, modest and friendly. They study one another. They look into each other's eyes. And, warmed by the sun and mellowed by the claret, they can't find anything in the other man's face to justify hatred, nothing, indeed, which doesn't inspire human affection, nothing incompatible in their languages any more, or in their particular way of scratching the nose or drinking wine. They really are exuding peace, and the world's desire for peace. And when their meeting is over, they shake hands in a most sincere brotherly fashion, and turn to smile and wave as they drive away. And the next day war breaks out. And so it is with us both at this moment. Our peoples, who have drawn aside, saying nothing while we have this interview, are not expecting us to win a victory over the inevitable. They have merely given us full powers, isolated here together, to stand above the catastrophe and taste the essential brotherhood of enemies. Taste it. It's a rare dish. Savour it. But that is all. One of the privileges of the great is to witness catastrophes from a terrace.

HECTOR: Do you think this is a conversation between enemies we are having?

ULYSSES: I should say a duet before the full orchestra. Because we have been created sensible and courteous, we can talk to each other, an hour or so before the war, in the way we shall talk to each other long after it's over, like old antagonists. We are merely having our reconciliation before the struggle instead of after it. That may be unwise. If one day one of us should have to kill the other, it might be as well if it wasn't a friend's face we recognized as the body dropped to the ground. But, as the universe well knows, we are going to fight each other.

HECTOR: The universe might be mistaken. One way to recognize error is the fact that it's universal.

ULYSSES: Let's hope so. But when destiny has brought up two nations, as for years it has brought up yours and mine, to a future of similar invention and authority, and given to each a different scale of values (as you and I saw just now, when we weighed pleasure against pleasure, conscience against conscience, even nature itself against nature): when the nation's architects and poets and painters have created for them opposing kingdoms of sound, and form, and subtlety, when we have a Trojan tile roof, a Theban arch, Phrygian red, Greek blue: the universe knows that destiny wasn't preparing alternative ways for civilization to flower. It was contriving the dance of death, letting loose the brutality and human folly which is all that the gods are really contented by. It's a mean way to contrive things, I agree. But we are Heads of State, you and I; we can say this between ourselves: it is Destiny's way of contriving things, inevitably.

HECTOR: And this time it has chosen to match Greece with Troy?

ULYSSES: This morning I was still in doubt. As soon as I stepped on to your landing stage I was certain of it.

HECTOR: You mean you felt yourself on enemy soil?

ULYSSES: Why will you always harp on the word enemy? Born enemies don't fight. Nations you would say were designed to go to war against each other – by their skins, their language, their smell: always jealous of each other, always hating each other – they're not the ones who fight. You will find the real antagonists in nations fate has groomed and made ready for the same war.

HECTOR: And you think we have been made ready for the Greek war?

ULYSSES: To an astonishing extent. Just as nature, when she foresees a struggle between two kinds of insects, equips them with weaknesses and weapons which correspond, so we, living well apart, unknown to ourselves, not even suspecting it, have both been gradually raised up to the level where war begins. All our weapons and habits correspond with each other and balance against each other like the beams of a gable. No other women in the world excite less brutality in us, or less desire, than your wives and daughters do; they give us a joy and an anguish of heart which is a sure sign of impending war between us. Doom has transfigured everything here with the colour of storm: your grave buildings shaking with shadow and fire, the neighing horses, figures disappearing into the dark of a colonnade: the future has never impressed me before with such startling clarity. There is nothing to be done. You're already living in the light of the Greek war.

HECTOR: And do the rest of the Greeks think this?

ULYSSES: What they think is no more reassuring. The rest of the Greeks think Troy is wealthy, her warehouses bulging, her soil prolific. They think that they, on the other hand, are living cramped on a rock. And your golden temples and golden wheatfields flashed from your promontories a signal our ships will never forget. It isn't very wise to have such golden gods and vegetables.

HECTOR: This is more like the truth, at last. Greece has chosen Troy for her prey. Then why a declaration of war? It would have been simpler to have taken Troy by surprise when I was away with the army. You would have had her without striking a blow.

ULYSSES: There's a kind of permission for war which can be given only by the world's mood and atmosphere, the feel of its pulse. It would have been madness to undertake a war without that permission. We didn't have it.

HECTOR: But you have it now.

ULYSSES: I think we do.

HECTOR: But why against us? Troy is famous for her arts, her justice, her humanity.

ULYSSES: A nation doesn't put itself at odds with its destiny by its crimes, but by its faults. Its army may be strong, its treasury well filled, its poets at the height of inspiration. But one day, why it is no one knows, because of some simple event, such as the citizens wantonly cutting down the trees, or their prince wickedly making off with a woman, or the children getting out of hand, the nation is suddenly lost. Nations, like men, die by imperceptible disorders. We recognize a doomed people by the way they sneeze or pare their nails. There's no doubt you carried off Helen badly.

HECTOR: What fairness of proportion can you see between the rape of one woman, and the possible destruction of a whole people, yours or mine, in war?

ULYSSES: We are speaking of Helen. You and Paris have made a great mistake about Helen. I've known her fifteen years, and watched her carefully. There's no doubt about it: she is one of the rare creatures destiny puts on the earth for its own personal use. They're apparently quite unimportant. It might be not even a person, but a small town, or a village: a little queen, or a child; but if you lay hands on them, watch out! It's very hard to know how to recognize one of these hostages of fate among all the other people and places. You haven't recognized it. You could have laid hands with impunity on our great admirals or one of our kings. Paris could have let himself go with perfect safety in a Spartan bed, or a Theban bed, with generous returns twenty times over; but he chose the shallowest brain, the hardest heart, the narrowest understanding of sex. And so you are lost.

HECTOR: We are giving Helen back to you.

ULYSSES: The insult to destiny can't be taken back.

HECTOR: What are we discussing, then? I'm beginning to see what is really behind your words. Admit it. You want our wealth! You had Helen carried off to give you an honourable pretext for war! I blush for Greece. She will be responsible and ashamed for the rest of time.

ULYSSES: Responsible and ashamed? Do you think so? The two words hardly agree. Even if we believed we were responsible for the war, all our generation would have to do would be to deny it, and lie, to appease the conscience of future generations. And we shall lie. We'll make that sacrifice.

HECTOR: Ah, well, the die is cast, Ulysses. On with the war! The more I hate it, the more I find growing in me an irresistible need to kill. If you won't help me, it were better you should leave here.

ULYSSES: Understand me, Hector; you have my help. Don't ask me to interpret fate. All I have tried to do is to read the world's hand, in the great lines of desert caravans, the wake of ships, and the track of migrant birds and wandering peoples. Give me your hand. There are lines there, too. We won't search to see if their lesson tells the same story. We'll suppose that these three little lines at the base of Hector's hand contradict the waves, the wings, and the furrows. I am inquisitive by nature, and not easily frightened. I'm quite willing to join issue with fate. I accept your offer of Helen. I will take her back to Menelaus. I've more than enough eloquence to convince a husband of his wife's virtue. I will even persuade Helen to believe it herself. And I'll leave at once, to avoid any chance of disturbance. Once back on my ship perhaps we can take the risk of running war on to the rocks.

HECTOR: Is this part of Ulysses' cunning, or his greatness?

ULYSSES: In this particular instance, I'm using my cunning against destiny, not against you. It's my first attempt, so I deserve some credit for it. I am sincere, Hector. If I wanted war, I should have asked for a ransom more precious to you than Helen. I am going now. But I can't shake off the feeling that the road from here to my ship is a long way.

HECTOR: My guard will escort you.

ULYSSES: As long as the road of a visiting king, when he knows there has been a threat against his life. Where are the assassins hiding? We're lucky if it's not in the heavens themselves. And the distance from here to the corner of the palace is a long way. A long way, taking this first step. Where is it going to carry me among all these perils? Am I going to slip and kill myself? Will part of the cornice fall down on me? It's all new stonework here; at any moment a stone may be dislodged. But courage. Let us go. (*He takes a first step.*)

HECTOR: Thank you, Ulysses.

ULYSSES: The first step is safely over. How many more?

HECTOR: Four hundred and sixty.

ULYSSES: Now the second! You know what made me decide to go, Hector?

HECTOR: Yes. Your noble nature.

ULYSSES: Not precisely. Andromache's eyelashes dance as my wife Penelope's do. (*He goes.*)

Enter Andromache and Cassandra.

HECTOR: Were you there all the time, Andromache?

ANDROMACHE: Let me take your arm. I've no more strength.

HECTOR: Did you hear what we said?

ANDROMACHE: Yes. I am broken.

HECTOR: You see, we needn't despair.

ANDROMACHE: We needn't despair for ourselves, perhaps. But for the world, yes. That man is terrible. All the unhappiness of the world is in me.

HECTOR: A moment or two more, and Ulysses will be on board. You see how fast he is travelling. You can follow his progress from here. There he is, on a level with the fountains. What are you doing?

ANDROMACHE: I haven't the strength any longer to hear any more. I am covering up my ears. I won't take my hands away until we know what our fate is to be.

HECTOR: Find Helen, Cassandra!

Ajax enters, more drunk than ever. He sees Andromache. Her back towards him.

CASSANDRA: Ulysses is waiting for you down at the harbour, Ajax. Helen will be brought to you there.

AJAX: Helen! To hell with Helen! This is the one I want to get my arms around.

CASSANDRA: Go away, Ajax. That is Hector's wife.

AJAX: Hector's wife! Bravo! I've always liked my friends' wives, my best friends' wives!

CASSANDRA: Ulysses is already half-way there. Hurry.

AJAX: Don't worry, my dear. She's got her hands over her ears. I can say what I like, she can't hear me. If I touched her, now, if I kissed her, certainly! But words she can't hear, what's the matter with that?

CASSANDRA: Everything is the matter with that. Go away, Ajax!

Ajax, while Cassandra tries to force him away from Andromache and Hector, slowly raises his javelin.

AJAX: Do you think so? Then I might as well touch her. Might as well kiss her. But chastely, always chastely, with your best friends' wives! What's the most chaste part of your wife, Hector, her neck? So much for her neck. Her ear has a pretty little look of chastity to me. So much for her ear. I'll tell you what I've always found the chastest thing about a woman . . . Let me alone, now; let me alone! She can't even hear when I kiss her . . . You're so cursed strong! All right, I'm going, I said I was going. Good-bye.

He goes. Hector imperceptibly lowers his javelin. At this moment Demokos bursts in.

DEMOKOS: What's this cowardice? You're giving Helen back? Trojans, to arms! They've betrayed us. Fall in! And your war-song is ready! Listen to your war-song!

HECTOR (*striking him*): Have that for your war-song!

DEMOKOS (*falling*): He has killed me!

HECTOR: The war isn't going to happen, Andromache!

He tries to take Andromache's hands from her ears: she resists, her eyes fixed on Demokos. The curtain which had begun to fall is lifted little by little.

ABNEOS: They have killed Demokos! Who killed Demokos?

DEMOKOS: Who killed me? Ajax! Ajax! Kill him!

ABNEOS: Kill Ajax!

HECTOR: He's lying. I am the man who struck him.

DEMOKOS: No. It was Ajax.

ABNEOS: Ajax has killed Demokos. Catch him! Punish him!

HECTOR: I struck you, Demokos, admit it! Admit it, or I'll put an end to you!

DEMOKOS: No, my dear Hector, my good dear Hector. It was Ajax. Kill Ajax!

CASSANDRA: He is dying, just as he lived, croaking like a frog.

ABNEOS: There. They have taken Ajax. There. They have killed him!

HECTOR (*drawing Andromache's hands away from her ears*): The war will happen.

The Gates of War slowly open, to show Helen kissing Troilus.

CASSANDRA: The Trojan poet is dead. And now the Grecian poet will have his word.

The curtain finally falls

NOTE

In the stage version at the Apollo Theatre the following passage was substituted for the dialogue between CASSANDRA, HELEN and PEACE on pages 97 and 98:

HELEN: Cassandra, you can see what I can see. You could have helped him to understand me.

CASSANDRA: He understands you only too clearly. And, besides, I see nothing; I never have seen anything, coloured or not. But I can feel the weight of every person who comes towards me. I know what is in store for them by the sensation of suffering which flows into my veins.

HELEN: In fact, you feel what I can see.

CASSANDRA: What I feel in Hector is a suffering too deep to be suffered. He may yet break the reflection in your mirror, Helen. He may have hands great enough to strangle the tiger as it springs.

HELEN: Do you suppose so?

CASSANDRA: There is always something more than one supposes.

Duel of Angels

Original title: *Pour Lucrèce*

First presented at the Théâtre Marigny on 4 November 1953 in a production by Jean-Louis Barrault.

First presented in England at the Theatre Royal, Newcastle-upon-Tyne, on 3 March 1958, with the following cast:

JOSEPH	Derek Nimmo
MARCELLUS	Peter Wyngarde
GILLY	Fiona Duncan
PAOLA	Vivien Leigh
ARMAND	Basil Hoskins
LUCILE	Claire Bloom
EUGÉNIE	Pauline Jameson
MACE-BEARER	Beaufoy Milton
BARBETTE	Freda Jackson
MARCELLUS'S SERVANT	Brian Harrison
MR JUSTICE BLANCHARD	Robin Bailey
CLERK OF THE COURT	Lawrence Davidson
MR JUSTICE BLANCHARD'S SERVANT	John Hart Dyke

CUSTOMERS AT THE CAFÉ

Sylvia Kay, Sally Home, Barbara Bolton, John Hart Dyke, Lawrence Davidson, Brian Harrison, David Maxwell, Lawrence Brooks

Directed by JEAN-LOUIS BARRAULT
Décor by ROGER FURSE

ACT ONE

*At Aix-en-Provence. About 1868. A summer's day. The terrace of
a tea-shop under the lime trees.*
Count Marcellus. Joseph. Customers.

JOSEPH: What would you like, sir?

MARCELLUS: What would I like, Joseph? I should like you to
tell me what Vice means.

JOSEPH: I left school too young to be able to tell you that, sir.

MARCELLUS: Make a guess. If someone mentions vice to you,
what do you imagine?

JOSEPH: We are not here to imagine things, sir; we're here to
serve our customers.

MARCELLUS: Then you'd better serve me with whatever goes
well with vice. Mr Justice Blanchard has just proclaimed in
open court that I am Vice, Joseph.

JOSEPH: I don't really know what to suggest I bring you, sir.
Though I always think a mixed ice goes quite well with anything. If you'll excuse me, sir, I'll refer to the manager.

Exit Joseph.

GILLY (*a flower-seller*): Would you like a flower, sir?

MARCELLUS: No, my dear. You haven't got the flower there
which Mr Justice Blanchard has prescribed for me.

GILLY: I've some camellias.

MARCELLUS: Mr Justice Blanchard has insisted that from now
on my buttonhole should carry an orchid streaked with
blood, stinking of corruption.

GILLY: Antirrhinums, I could manage. That's the nearest we
can get to orchids in Aix. It won't take me five minutes to get
them for you, sir.

MARCELLUS: Splendid. Bring them to my house.

GILLY: I can't do that, sir. Mr Justice Blanchard has forbidden
any girls under sixteen, especially flower-girls and laundry-
maids, to go to the houses of unmarried gentlemen alone, sir.

MARCELLUS: Bring your mother. We can install her in the kitchen.

GILLY: My mother's in prison. Mr Justice Blanchard sent her there, for taking some letters from the city treasurer to the prefect's wife.

Enter Paola with her husband Armand.

PAOLA: Good afternoon, Vice! Shall we sit next to Vice, Armand?

MARCELLUS: So you've heard about it already.

PAOLA: Beauty is always the first to hear about the sins of the world.

ARMAND: I was in court.

MARCELLUS: I understand he took me to task in no uncertain terms.

ARMAND: Smote you hip and thigh. He was sentencing that girl who used to visit you, who killed her baby.

PAOLA: And he declared our dear city of Aix to be as bad as Sodom or Gomorrah.

MARCELLUS: But what did he say about me? Tell me what he said.

ARMAND: He said they can't imprison you for debt, because you're too rich. They can't run you out of the district for being a nuisance, because you're too wily. No family is going to complain about you, because you would threaten them with blackmail. But he took it upon himself to execrate your name at the bar of justice, and to point out your face for anyone to spit at who cares to.

MARCELLUS: A very detailed report. To spit at, he said?

ARMAND: That's what he said. He also mentioned debauchery. He also mentioned vice.

MARCELLUS: Precisely in that tone of voice.

ARMAND: I've been an actor in my time. I know how to copy an inflection. He said he had a mission to perform: to see that this town didn't run downhill to perdition, and since you stand for a kind of symbol of the town, he would start his attack with you.

MARCELLUS: I might be listening to the voice of any husband in Aix. I might be listening to you.

ARMAND: I don't mind you thinking so.

PAOLA: Oh, come now, Armand. You don't really side with these hypocrites!

ARMAND: My dear Paola, I'm a husband. You mustn't expect me to congratulate a seducer. You'd better get out of Aix, Marcellus. And I suggest that you hurry.

Joseph returns.

JOSEPH: Vice is the natural propensity to evil, sir. We have a dictionary in the office. And the manager advises sherry with a drop of grenadine. That was the strongest thing he remembers them serving at the Café Anglais. But he would like you to be so very good as to choose another table. This one is reserved, sir.

MARCELLUS: For whom, Joseph?

JOSEPH: I don't know, sir.

MARCELLUS: You do know, Joseph. I heard the hesitation. For whom?

JOSEPH: For Madame Lionel Blanchard.

MARCELLUS: For Mr Justice Blanchard's wife?

PAOLA: Of course, Marcellus. The wife of the man who has given you all this publicity. She comes here every day.

MARCELLUS: The gift of an opportunity; the duel can begin. Have you got a drum, Joseph?

JOSEPH: We have this Egyptian gong, sir.

MARCELLUS: Strike it.

ARMAND: Bad behaviour again, Marcellus!

MARCELLUS: Maybe; but beautifully expressed, as you shall see!

Joseph beats the gong. Marcellus rises.

CUSTOMER: Joseph, we shall all have to leave. That's enough of this racket.

ANOTHER CUSTOMER: If we have to have Vice among us, at least he ought to keep quiet.

MARCELLUS: Forgive me, and stay where you are, honest inhabitants of Aix. Vice has a mission to perform today, and no man alive is going to make him relinquish it. His mission is to introduce Virtue to you; Virtue is on her way. You will see her in the flesh, sitting enthroned in this chair. Give her your careful attention. She can revive your drooping senses far more effectively than Vice can. You will see her, Monsieur Oscar, tasting an ice with a tongue which has never ventured beyond the kiss of a dutiful wife. You will hear her, Monsieur Julius, speaking with a mouth which has never told an untruth. You will watch her picking up a biscuit with fingers which have never strayed away in the dark, my dear Armand.

ARMAND: Kindly leave me out of this.

MARCELLUS: But above all, virtuous wives and excellent husbands of Aix, her coming here will throw light on your own marriages. Wherever this lady goes, life takes on the agreeable charm of the Last Judgement. I don't know how it is, considering she never listens to gossip, but one touch of human frailty and she knows it, and, as far as she's concerned, that's the end of you. Watch her closely. I can tell you, she is absolutely unmerciful. If she refuses to acknowledge an acquaintance, you can be quite sure that acquaintance has found a lover . . .

ARMAND: Here she is, I think, Marcellus. You'd better shut up.

MARCELLUS: If she suddenly refuses to speak to some poor husband, his wife has betrayed him; and any husband so betrayed she holds personally responsible.

PAOLA: That's enough, Marcellus. You're being tiresome.

MARCELLUS: Don't hesitate. Use this touchstone to show you what you are yourselves. Try asking her for the sugar; if you've just been reading the *Decameron* she won't pass it. Pick up her scarf; she won't accept it from you if she knows you've got a collection of rather light-hearted engravings. Here she is. Go and meet her, Joseph. You'll be able to tell from the way she greets you whether you're deceived or deceiving.

PAOLA: Let's change our table. Let's go over there.

ARMAND: Why?

MARCELLUS: Here she comes, to take over from me. Vice and Virtue are meeting face to face for the first time. Her expression will tell you, fellow inhabitants of Aix, what part I'm expected to play for the rest of the afternoon.

Lucile enters with Eugénie.

This is your table, madam. I have been keeping it for you.

LUCILE (*smiling at him*): Thank you.

Marcellus goes to a distant table.

Good afternoon, Joseph. You're bowing very low today.

JOSEPH: Slightly lower than yesterday, madam. I have good reason to.

LUCILE: But you'll bring us our ices, won't you, Joseph?

JOSEPH: I shall see they're even colder than yesterday, madam.

LUCILE: And the chocolate a little hotter, I hope.

JOSEPH: The ice freezing, madam. The chocolate boiling.

LUCILE: Perfect.

JOSEPH (*coming back to her*): My wife makes the wafers.

LUCILE: Thank her very much. Remember me to her, Joseph.

JOSEPH: Thank you, madam, I will! I shall kiss her, madam. My goodness, I'm delighted.

Exit Joseph.

LUCILE: Are you sulking, Eugénie?

EUGÉNIE: Yes, I am. I'm vexed that you didn't let Guy come with us.

LUCILE: I never feel quite at ease with him. I'm afraid I can't help it.

EUGÉNIE: There's beginning to be a lot of talk in the town about your likes and dislikes. They're so extraordinary.

LUCILE: What do you mean?

EUGÉNIE: Well, you don't seem to have any particular aversion to thieves. Or drunkards; I've seen you being most pleasant to them. Even that murderer we saw being arrested; you looked as though you pitied him.

LUCILE: He was much to be pitied. And my husband is the judge. One judge in the family is enough.

EUGÉNIE: You can face any of these faults and crimes quite cheerfully, be talkative, and gracious, and in the best of spirits. Then you suddenly freeze and clench your teeth and refuse to speak, as though your flesh had been turned to stone.

LUCILE: But you know why.

EUGÉNIE: Yes, I do. Someone in love had just happened to go past.

LUCILE: That's far from the truth.

EUGÉNIE: Some enchanting woman was going by on her way to see her lover. Or a young man waved to us when he was running to fetch a letter from the poste restante.

LUCILE: Are you lying to hurt me, or just for the sake of lying?

EUGÉNIE: A woman can be swathed up to the neck, as modestly as possible. You still manage to discover the marks of unlawful kissing hidden away on her body. It's as though when you looked at a wealth of family jewellery your eyes saw nothing except the fake. You're making this town impossible to live in.

LUCILE: What does it have to do with the town?

EUGÉNIE: Aix was like a town of love before you came here. At least half the road these people took through life was dedicated to love. And what a beautiful pattern their footsteps made, lacing and interlacing! If you followed any man or woman in Aix at any time of the day or night they would bring you to where love was.

LUCILE: That's a strange name to give it.

EUGÉNIE: The right one. Desire, pursuit, jealousy, blessing, despair – love can be called by any of them.

LUCILE: Not by me. Love is called love, and no other name will do.

EUGÉNIE: It gave a great many privileges to this town: husbands were trusting, mothers were careful to shut their eyes. Even the smallest, ordinary pleasures came brilliantly to life because they happened in a world of love. As though the climate of Aix bred love like a fever, and nobody minded. We left typhoid and cholera to Marseilles; here we had love. And then you came along, you and your judge of a husband, Lucile and Lionel.

LUCILE: Lucile and Lionel, who simply love each other, without complication.

EUGÉNIE: They arrived from Limousin, the country which has bred more Popes and fewer lovers than any other in the world. And Lionel has been a success, both as a jealous husband and an upright judge. From the first month he was here he picked up the threads of every affair in the town. And his homilies rang out, his sermons against public licence, and off to the pillory went all the happy people who were guilty. People laugh at him, because they understand what he doesn't understand. But you, Lucile, really did bring calamity with you.

LUCILE: I brought calamity?

Joseph returns.

JOSEPH: Your ices, madam.

LUCILE: Thanks.

JOSEPH: My wife sends you these wafers with her compliments.

LUCILE: Thanks.

JOSEPH: My wife –

EUGÉNIE: Stop worrying us about your wife, Joseph.

JOSEPH: Oh, dear! It's what I was afraid of!

Exit Joseph.

EUGÉNIE: You've given the taste of hell to innocent, carefree pleasure. They believe you're guilty of reintroducing original sin; you needn't suppose you're another Lucrece. You're the angel of evil.

LUCILE: And yet it's all so simple.

EUGÉNIE: What is it you see about these people which suddenly turns you to stone?

LUCILE: I see insects and reptiles on them.

149

EUGÉNIE: A peculiar gift.

LUCILE: I realize perfectly well that if I were a saint I shouldn't despise them for it. But I can't help it. On every incontinent person I see a creature.

EUGÉNIE: Always the same creature?

LUCILE: No. It may be slimy, or it may be crawling. It comes out of their mouths, and runs over their bodies.

EUGÉNIE: And all this time you have been seeing one on my friend Guy?

LUCILE: A little one. A very little toad. Hardly more than a tadpole.

EUGÉNIE: In his hand, when you refused to shake hands with him?

LUCILE: No; on his mouth.

EUGÉNIE: You haven't come from Limousin; you've come out of the Middle Ages. And did you see one on Clotilda when you hurried past without speaking to her?

LUCILE: There was a maggot in the corner of her eye.

EUGÉNIE: Can you say this without laughing? And if there should happen to be someone you think well of, what do you see on them?

LUCILE: I see their senses lying transparent under their skin. Their eyes are like clear water. Their bones like ivory.

EUGÉNIE: Your morality is uncommonly physical, it seems to me.

LUCILE: Our bodies are what God has given into our keeping, Eugénie. He takes care of our souls himself.

EUGÉNIE: I'm surprised that you've noticed your body. Have you really been daring enough to look at it in the mirror? Don't you tie yourself up in a sack when you sleep with the Judge?

LUCILE: I have a great respect for my body. It is healthy, loyal, and sensible. I keep well away from that common burial ground which promiscuity leads to. Who are you smiling at?

EUGÉNIE: At Paola. Acknowledge her. She's waving to you.

LUCILE: Never.

EUGÉNIE: Don't be difficult; please, Lucile. Paola is great fun, and very beautiful. You needn't wave, but incline your head to beauty.

LUCILE: Beauty which takes a lover isn't there for me to see.

EUGÉNIE: A slug is crawling out of her ear, I suppose?

LUCILE: Praying mantises; thousands of them.

EUGÉNIE: Her husband is smiling at you, very insistently.

LUCILE: A man whose wife takes a lover doesn't smile; he makes an insulting grimace.

EUGÉNIE: But he doesn't know anything about it. You know Armand. Only this morning you were speaking very well of him. If he guessed he would kill himself, or kill somebody.

LUCILE: Why, everything must surely shout it at him. If he can't detect it in the whole atmosphere of his house, then he's as guilty and contemptible as all the rest are.

EUGÉNIE: Be careful. He'll see it in your face.

LUCILE: My face makes it useless to try to lie. That's why sometimes I can look at it in the mirror.

EUGÉNIE: Please, Lucile; do acknowledge them. He has gone quite pale, and Paola is furious. Armand knows perfectly well what makes you refuse to recognize a friend, what it is that strikes you dumb in front of a husband.

LUCILE: Dumb, deaf, and blind.

EUGÉNIE: He is coming over to us. Say something to him, just a word or two. I'm not asking you to touch him.

LUCILE: There isn't any difference; if I speak it's as if I touched him. And anyway, after this conversation love is the only word on my tongue at the moment. Don't ask me to speak to him.

EUGÉNIE: Poor Armand! He always talks like a lyric poet, and now here he comes, searching for his death.

Armand reaches the table.

ARMAND: My respects to you, dear madam.

EUGÉNIE: Thank you, dear Armand. We accept them.

ARMAND: My respects, Eugénie . . . You also accept them, I hope, Madame Blanchard? It is wonderful to see you together, two women endued with the same grace.

EUGÉNIE: We go to the same dressmaker, my dear friend.

ARMAND: Really wonderful: as though grace couldn't completely express itself without the help of two such different souls and bodies.

EUGÉNIE: You could hardly say more if you wrote a sonnet to us, Armand.

ARMAND: But it's not so satisfactory to think it should have provided only one voice between you. Two mouths, but one voice.

EUGÉNIE: Some men would think that was a very reasonable arrangement for women.

ARMAND: And yet I wish that your friend could have told me why she doesn't make any acknowledgement when Paola waves to her.

EUGÉNIE: I don't think she saw her.

ARMAND: Then I wish she could tell me why Paola has become invisible to her, twenty feet away, in a red dress, and smiling all over her face in this direction. Paola has just given the biggest smile of her life.

EUGÉNIE: You should be very thankful that my friend is so lost in abstraction. Otherwise she would see the most charming man in Aix becoming importunate.

ARMAND: I'm only saying what all Aix is feeling. The town is deeply disturbed by Madame Blanchard's attacks of blindness and deafness.

EUGÉNIE: We're very sorry; there's no cure, I'm afraid.

ARMAND: I think there is. They say that Madame Blanchard would talk from dawn to dusk without a pause, and even chatter on into her dreams, if every couple in the town were perfect.

EUGÉNIE: I don't understand what you mean.

ARMAND: Yes, you do; but you're the one entrusted to speak, so you're also the one entrusted to lie. And as I have to use you as an interpreter, tell your friend that I'm begging her to break the silence. If she doesn't speak to me, she's forcing me to believe that either I'm an unfaithful husband or a deceived one. But I know I'm a faithful husband . . .

EUGÉNIE: Are you sure of that?

ARMAND: You can't wave the charges away. I've been meaning for a long time to shout from the rooftops that I love my wife. It isn't often done, to trumpet abroad a husband's love for his wife, particularly in Aix. I'm grateful to your friend for giving me the chance.

EUGÉNIE: Don't shout so loud. Your wife is looking.

ARMAND: I hope she can hear me. I love my wife in and above everything. Don't smile. You don't have to speak simply when you make a public confession; you want words that resound. Thanks to her, I love everything. Thanks to her, I have everything. The world, and time, and space, have surrendered to me by way of her. In her I move, in her I breathe. For me she is every minute on the clock. She's the sun in the sky; the whole solar system. My wife is the only reason I love at all. And now perhaps you can see why I should like Madame Blanchard to speak to me . . .

EUGÉNIE: You're insisting so much. It discourages conversation.

ARMAND: . . . to say any word she likes. Let Madame Blanchard mention the weather to me. Let her ask me if it's going to be fine. She will see then. Eugénie, the sky will never have looked so wonderfully promising.

EUGÉNIE: We were talking about the weather when you came over to us. There's nothing more to say about it.

ARMAND: I'm not asking for charity, I don't want her to lie.

EUGÉNIE: Now listen, Armand! At last a woman has come into this distracted world who refuses to speak when she has nothing to say, who likes to be allowed to become a statue if she wants to, and you pester her with idiotic questions!

ARMAND: Even a statue would answer me, at the moment.

EUGÉNIE: If Lucile gave in to you, it would be because she thought you were stupid. All she could say to you would be that you're like everybody else, pigheaded and egotistical, incapable of understanding the heart and the silence it longs to have.

ARMAND: Very well: I withdraw. Madame Blanchard needn't be silent any longer . . . Thank you, madam.

He goes back to his wife.

EUGÉNIE: You can now congratulate yourself that you kept the word love safe in your mouth like an acid drop.

LUCILE: It hasn't melted.

EUGÉNIE: And suppose now he should slap Paola's face in public, would you condescend to tell him he had done well? Or suppose he should kill her?

LUCILE: There's no fear of that. He was acting a part.

EUGÉNIE: But she certainly isn't. And she's going to make sure that you know that. Poor Armand! What have you been doing this morning to make you so cruel to husbands?

LUCILE: Nothing much. I kissed my husband, and held him in my arms when he set off on circuit to Draguignan. I washed a dinner service of old Marseilles china. I read two metaphysical poems. Then I sat down and wrote a letter to my husband, telling him that I had washed the dinner service and read the poems.

EUGÉNIE: Here he is back again.

ARMAND: Yes. I'm back. When men have been talking to a woman they want to see again, they leave their gloves or their stick behind. I left my life on your table, my dear Eugénie, my entire life.

EUGÉNIE: You left your gloves as well. They would have been quite enough.

ARMAND (*taking the gloves*): Thank you.

EUGÉNIE: And now I suppose you want to look for your life?

ARMAND: I've already seen it. My wife hasn't deceived me.

EUGÉNIE: Dear heaven, what are we talking about?

ARMAND: About my wife. She hasn't deceived me. I've come back to ask Madame Blanchard why she won't speak.

EUGÉNIE: Madame Blanchard has to recite two metaphysical poems at the Archbishop's reception tomorrow afternoon. This is the only time she has to go over them in her mind. Don't worry her.

ARMAND: I see. And I'm sure Madame Blanchard has also sworn to count up to a million, and she would have to start all over again if she interrupted herself. But my wife hasn't deceived me.

EUGÉNIE: Then she should have done. You're impossible.

ARMAND: I'm a visionary, in a way. I've often foreseen death, and accidents, and people's good fortune. But I've never felt any apprehensiveness when I thought of Paola. Very often I hear myself talking out loud to myself in the street, and I tell myself hard truths which had never occurred to me before. But I've never heard myself say: "Your wife has a lover, Armand. You have a wife who has a lover." And that's because she hasn't.

EUGÉNIE: If you don't stop, Armand, we shall have to leave.

ARMAND: No, you won't. Madame Blanchard has no intention of leaving. She's not the sort of person to beat a retreat, or compromise. She keeps her opinions to herself, even if it kills her. But there's no reason why she should; and I'll tell her why. I am very like her. I shrink away from unpleasantness and uncertainty, and, like her, I'm speechless when I come across deception and the sins of the flesh. I know I might very well overlook an excess of sentiment or imagination in my wife, but never a fault of her body. I've just been testing this now, sitting beside her. She drank her coffee like an innocent woman; she broke her biscuit like a faithful wife. She took a sip of water like a woman who had never known, or seen, or touched any man except her husband.

EUGÉNIE: Who doubts it? No one ever questioned it!

ARMAND: I certainly don't. Besides, if my wife wasn't faithful, I should have known it an hour ago. I go back to my house once a day unexpectedly and I quietly open the door, not to take Paola by surprise, of course, God forbid, but to surprise the house itself. And that's what I did just now. My proof is less than an hour old. All I surprised was a complete innocence. You know I collect furniture; and I know if anything were ever wrong, those beautiful, various pieces, the rosewood and acacia-wood, and so on, would seem to me to be all made of the same dreary material, common wood, like the common flesh of mankind. But just now the walnut still came from the walnut tree, the rosewood from the rose. And in my collection of Turkish bric-à-brac the coiling and glittering snakes of pure silver were pure silver still, and still lighted my heart. The tranquil waters of Europe still flowed for me, the peaceful waters of Asia still sang in my ear. So you see, Eugénie . . .

EUGÉNIE: So don't insist, Armand.

ARMAND: I'm not insisting. I've always taken care not to insist. But there's one other thing I want to tell Madame Blanchard, which she doesn't know. I created Paola. I created her temperament, her wit, and all her ways of living. She has read nothing but what I have read, and seen only the pictures and the landscapes which I showed her. Not because she wasn't capable of doing these things for herself; in every way she's both gifted and original. But she chose to let herself be created by me. She eats and drinks according to my taste, dresses and undresses according to my taste. I made her days, her nights, even her flesh. It would be wise of Madame Blanchard to believe that I don't create a woman just to be betrayed by her.

EUGÉNIE: My dear Armand, do be serious. Sit down here, next to us. Let me offer you an ice.

ARMAND: There; that's all. I won't ask Madame Blanchard to say a word. You were quite right just now, Eugénie. It's quite natural that a woman should suddenly find it tiresome to speak; tiresome and complicated.

EUGÉNIE: You're becoming quite sensible.

ARMAND: Good-bye, madam. I am going back to fidelity, love, and happiness. I shall never leave them again.

EUGÉNIE: Till tomorrow, Armand.

ARMAND (turning back): However, there's one favour I should like to ask of Madame Blanchard. It may be impossibly difficult for her to speak, but it's easy enough to drink. Perfectly pleasant to raise a glass of water to the mouth. If Madame Blanchard agrees to tell me, without words, that

I'm right, let her simply raise her glass to her lips. May I tell
her that it's a very hot day, and she may enjoy it.

EUGÉNIE: Till tomorrow, Armand.

*Armand looks at Lucile, who does not drink. He goes away. As
soon as he has gone, Lucile unconsciously raises her glass to her lips.
Armand, still looking at her, sees this, and his face lights up. She
breaks the glass. Armand closes his eyes – confounded.*

You know what you're doing, don't you? You're stirring
up scandal, and a tragic drama. Armand was a magnificent
peacock with a hundred blind eyes in his tail. Now you're
making those eyes able to see.

LUCILE: Good. I hope they see everything.

EUGÉNIE: Putting a husband on his guard is like letting loose
the sorcerer's apprentice. In a flash Armand is going to see
every one of Paola's lovers, one for each eye. He will ruin
her, destroy her completely.

LUCILE: If she deserves it, where's the harm?

EUGÉNIE: Life is very hard for women like Paola. What they
would really like is to be virgin for each new lover. But they
have twenty loves, and only one body.

LUCILE: They have twenty bodies, and no love whatsoever.

EUGÉNIE: It maddens me to listen to you professing virtue in
a tea-shop, like a martyr professing his faith in the arena. It's
in bad taste, and with a tigress like Paola, it's dangerous.

LUCILE: You make me sound ridiculous when you say "virtue".
What have I said that has anything to do with being virtuous?

EUGÉNIE: Well, purity, if you like.

LUCILE: A beautiful word.

EUGÉNIE: Words have no connexions with all this.

LUCILE: For me they have. And I will tell you which words;
words like fountain, spring-water, crystal, and clarity. Don't
try and make me pity a disloyal wife and an unperceiving
husband, when there are words like truth and innocence.
You should imitate me a little, trust less to your thoughts and
more to language. That's why I can be glad to open my eyes

every morning. A flight of pure words lifts me into the sunshine.

EUGÉNIE: The word love isn't so ugly.

LUCILE: I'm very sure it isn't. Tell Armand so. I have cleansed it for him; you will see the strength it has now.

A Stout Man has got up from his table, and crosses to the two women. He drops on one knee beside them, and pretends to fasten his shoe-lace.

MAN: Help me to speak to you without being noticed, ladies. I'm the mace-bearer at the commercial court. This is very serious.

EUGÉNIE: Pretend to be searching for a gold piece.

MAN: I'd better look for a franc. It would seem more natural.

EUGÉNIE: Well? What is it?

MAN: Madame Blanchard, do speak to M. Armand. He's a very admirable man. You're killing him.

EUGÉNIE: It may be here, under the table.

MAN: What may, Madame Eugénie?

EUGÉNIE: Not my nose, your franc . . . Go on.

MAN: Madame Paola had an enemy once before, someone as beautiful as you are, who tried to take away her husband.

EUGÉNIE: But that isn't what we are doing.

MAN: You are. You're not taking him away for yourself, but you're taking him away from her. The person I'm referring to had to suffer for it. Someone unknown saw that she was well punished. It wouldn't have been surprising if her body had been scarred for life, if only one cheek and one eye had been left for her to look at in the mirror.

EUGÉNIE: Is this all you have to say?

MAN: By no means. I could tell you three other similar stories. But my back is breaking. It's most difficult, finding a franc you haven't lost. Ah, here it is. Many thanks, ladies. (*He goes.*)

EUGÉNIE: You heard that. Now, please. Armand will come back again. Everything that man said about Paola is true. She's inexorable. Speak to her husband. Or else let us leave here.

LUCILE: That man came just at the right moment. Otherwise I might have left.

EUGÉNIE: You mean you insist on staying.

LUCILE: Don't you ever feel that you've been given sometimes a direct order, something wills you to go to the house-keeper's room when you were really going to the drawing-room or up to the attic? My natural instinct now is to go home; there's some jam to be made and the laundry to see to. But my secret orders tell me to stay where I am.

EUGÉNIE: All right, let's stay, then. We shall discover what part obstinacy plays in this sad world.

LUCILE: We shall discover what part dignity plays in the human scheme.

Armand re-enters.

ARMAND: Madame Blanchard has found her voice again, I notice. The metaphysical poems have been rehearsed. She has counted up to a million. So I've come back.

EUGÉNIE: As we see. For the third time.

ARMAND: That's not many. I've seen a cat that was being drowned come back to shore twelve times, in spite of the sticks. Men haven't got the same tenacity. There will be no fourth time.

EUGÉNIE: My friend was showing you that a woman can be just as obstinate as a man, and more. You have lost. Let's call the game finished.

ARMAND: Well, Madame Blanchard spoke. And her voice was charming. But I'm sorry she did. When I sat over there listening to her, I noticed an imperfection in my wife which I had never noticed before. I always thought Paola had a gentle voice; low and gentle. But Paola's voice is hard, rasping. I used to think how firm and beautiful her lips were when she spoke, a heavenly horizontal. But they're not. They twist, and snap. Until today she sang like a lark; but what sort of croaking raven will she be tonight, I wonder.

EUGÉNIE: This was what my friend was trying to spare you when she wouldn't speak. So much the worse for you.

ARMAND: Then it was just as wrong for your friend to look at me. Madame Blanchard has eyes which have shown me that Paola's eyes aren't velvet, as I thought they were, but more like steel. I'm thankful I haven't felt Madame Blanchard's hand, or what would become of Paola's skin, which has always seemed to make the days and nights pass over me smooth as silk. A few minutes ago I touched it. It was still smooth, but it sweated a little – from fear, I think.

EUGÉNIE: If you won't leave now, Lucile, I shall go alone. This is sheer cruelty.

ARMAND: And yet Paola was so very dear to me until this morning. Madame Blanchard can have no idea what her tenderness used to be. I can remember so many things, which are very revealing. The care she took not to wake me; how she would slip into my arms without disturbing me when she came back from those solitary midnight visits she so loved making, to a church where the incense had the smell of tobacco; I noticed how the smell of it clung to her. And how, when it rained, her shoes would still be miraculously dry, because one of the saints had carried her home. It was a church where they gave red roses to the faithful, and she always chose the two most perfect roses to put in a vase by my side. I could smell the scent of them all through the night. And how brave she was, how she would hide from me the scratches and bruises she was so often giving herself. She would bruise her shoulders, and her breasts . . . just like a child . . . Sometimes even her belly. Oh God, I don't know!

EUGÉNIE (*getting up*): You're both going mad, both of you, you who can't stop talking, and my friend who refuses to speak at all; you're both losing your senses.

ARMAND: Not at all. On the contrary. It seems to me I'm finding them again. Give the devil his due. A clear vision; a twofold vision. Behind Madame Blanchard I can see an angel, her exact counterpart, suffering herself to be silent, forming a word with her lips, the unexpected word of friendship. And behind my wife a kind of monster, with drooping eyelids, yet looking so like her, and speaking the strange word "hatred".

EUGÉNIE : Are you contented now, Lucile ? This is your doing.

ARMAND : Yes, her doing. Or rather, not her doing. Because I've been watching my wife and I know she has lied to me.

EUGÉNIE : Do you see a crawling creature on me, Lucile ? You don't, I think. And that's because your peculiar gift is absolutely false. I have a lover. Good-bye.

Exit Eugénie.

ARMAND : I'm glad she has gone. You didn't speak because she was here, isn't that so ? And, because she was here, I talked too much, isn't that it ? She has a lover. What can we do ? Human beings are human beings. Whether it's a great herd of stags coming away from their offices at six, or out of their clubs and cafés at eight; or a great herd of females collected together in the wash-house or the tea-shop, what can we do ? The human animal is promiscuous. What I find so unjust is that I should have the feeling of having failed, or of having killed something. If the innocent are to suffer remorse, the guilty, presumably, should feel aggrieved. It's the worst possible solution.

PAOLA (*from her table*): Armand!

ARMAND : I came into this place with a young, faithful, beautiful wife; with memories of days which were happy, without spot or blemish; I leave with a graceless wife, whose looks have already gone; with years behind me of being fooled and humiliated. A splendid afternoon's work. I congratulate you. An anonymous silence is worth more than all the anonymous letters that were ever written.

PAOLA (*still from her table*): Armand!

ARMAND : She's calling me. She doesn't hear how harsh her voice is.

LUCILE (*turning to him with tears in her eyes*): Now you must listen to me – I do beg of you to listen!

ARMAND : Well ? I'm listening.

LUCILE : You haven't understood what my silence meant.

ARMAND: Have you been silent? It seems to me that we've told each other everything. It's the one profitable thing to have come out of the day. Happiness, misery, men, women: you've told me everything.

LUCILE: Someone told me you had spoken ill of my husband. That is why I've been reserved with you. I wasn't for a moment thinking of Paola.

ARMAND: A lie can be a very lovely thing, when a truthful woman tells it. I should like to see how far you can take it. To ask you to swear that Paola is faithful to me.

LUCILE: I'm quite ready to. What did you say about my husband at the club the day before yesterday?

ARMAND: I said that virtue was the weakness of strong generals, and the strength of weak magistrates.

LUCILE: Don't you think that was infamous? Now leave me. I won't say another word. Go away. Will you please go?

ARMAND: I'm not going back to the house today. I'm afraid of it.

Paola has got up, and is coming towards them.

PAOLA: Armand, angel?

ARMAND: Yes?

PAOLA: Angel, go and fetch me my wrap; I'm cold. You wouldn't mind slipping back to the house for it?

ARMAND: All right.

Exit Armand.

PAOLA (*to Lucile*): Will you condescend to speak to me?

LUCILE: That depends on the question.

PAOLA: No question; some information. I've come to tell you what you are.

LUCILE: I already know. I'm someone who can't bear women like you.

PAOLA: Even simpler than that. You're a woman who loves men.

LUCILE: That may be, when they've earned the right to be called men.

PAOLA: Like Charlemagne, for instance? Or Alexander? Or

that saint who took such care of the children? I've forgotten his name.

LUCILE: You haven't forgotten it. It's avoiding you.

PAOLA: Much good may it do it. But I'm more honest with myself; I can see them and judge them, without having to make great men out of them first.

LUCILE: One visits where one is received.

PAOLA: Be frank with me. What about other men, such as that swimmer you saw dive naked into the sea the other day: or the tenor we heard singing in *Aïda* last Thursday, who seemed to be moulded to his tights? Are they men to you, or not? What place do shoulders, and biceps, and thighs take in your vocabulary?

LUCILE: I've no idea.

PAOLA: You're thirty years old. You will soon find out. When men give themselves away to us: their footsteps on the pavement at night, letting us guess their weight; or their shadows in the moonlight showing us how insubstantial they are; or their voices coming up from the street, loud or gentle; what does all this mean to you? What do you make of it?

LUCILE: Shadows, footsteps, voices. Nothing more than that.

PAOLA: You're lying. They make your life. They're what you love.

LUCILE: Thank you for letting me know.

PAOLA: No thanks to me. You're a fairly rare type, but not unheard of. You're one of the women who never get used to living among millions of male bodies and souls. Day and night you're astonished at being a woman. Your reserve, and apparent modesty, come from this inability to take your sex for granted. You're curious about the woman you are, and at the same time rather frightened. You look at her in the mirror without ever getting to know her. When you're alone it's as though you'd made a shy arrangement to meet her; you move anxiously towards her when you're in bed . . . But that's not how you feel about men; men to you are clear, complete, and male, in body and spirit; and this game of virtue you play is nothing but affectation.

LUCILE: You describe yourself very well.

PAOLA: It's no description of me. I'm the complete opposite. I can never see or love more than one man. Not always the same one, I admit; I change him, but I love no one else. Not another man exists in the world. When he is with me, the rest are invisible, gone clean out of existence. When I love, every ship sails the sea without sailors, carriages travel without coachmen, the cakes in this shop make their own way up from the kitchen. In the confessional I'm given absolution by an echo. I watch other women dancing in a void, taking emptiness by the hand, laughing and chattering with what has no existence; because the only man who has any substance, flesh, or blood, is in my arms.

LUCILE: Does your husband also go clean out of existence?

PAOLA: My husband? No. He is still there, an obsession, a vague centre of my consciousness, the agreeable obsession who is my husband, like a memory which we don't turn to because we're so occupied with the present time. A companion, more shadow than flesh, who has my everyday life in his keeping. My interests, and habits, and likes, and dislikes are all safely in his care; my conversation on his lips, with everything I shall urgently need on the day I give up my latest lover; so when that awful day comes, the first man to emerge will be my husband. He will immediately become substantial, and encourage all the other men to come gradually out of the void where I had banished them. That's why I hold on to my husband. And now you know why I don't intend to let you separate us. Where should we find our next lover, without a husband to put men back into the world again?

LUCILE: This is absolutely horrifying!

PAOLA: A respectable remark, but humbug, if I may say so. Your own husband means even less to you than that.

LUCILE: We won't bring my husband into this.

PAOLA: However hard you may try to put the head of Solomon on to the judge, you don't change his body, which means nothing to you at all.

LUCILE: Wicked woman!

PAOLA: Well done. You spit with great charm, like a shocked schoolgirl. Your husband: it makes me laugh to think of him stirring up the woman in you for some other man's benefit. Lionel presenting you to Bertrand, or Jean-Paul, or Guy.

LUCILE: You know a number of Christian names.

PAOLA: Why, you let him go away; of course you don't love your husband. Every week, four times in a month, you're willing to let him go on circuit while you lie in an empty bed, perfectly contented and comfortable, suffering the worst evil that can happen to any woman in love: the absence of the lover. If you could have seen your look of calm well-being when you came in just now, you would have known that your husband meant nothing at all to you.

LUCILE: Oh, Lionel, my dear, forgive me for talking to this woman.

PAOLA: . . . who is teaching you the truth about a woman. Oh, Lionel, my dear, take as much time as you like on your journey! When you're away you're still close to me! . . . Completely untrue! Absence is absence; death, in fact. If someone I love is going away, if only for a day or an hour, I hold him to me, and cry out as though breath was leaving me; I hide his shoes. I make furious faces out of the window at him as he goes away, and insult him. You stand at the window and smile. When his weight is lifted off me, the weight of the world descends. But you breathe freely at last.

LUCILE: I hate you.

PAOLA: Hating another woman doesn't make you love your husband. And now listen to me. There's one thing that we won't leave undecided, and I've come to warn you of it.

LUCILE: Who is "we"? Are you speaking for some society?

PAOLA: Yes, I am. For all women. We believe that the worst crime any woman can commit is to go over to the side of the men. The one inviolable pact since the creation of the world, has been this agreement between women. And the woman who breaks it is bound for disaster. Man is simple. The only thing he demands from us is peace and quiet, to be left to play with his horses, and his work, and his money, and his own self-importance. He doesn't ask to live a real life, or to nurse his real passions, or to be a reality, in the sense a woman is. He wants to go on with his game of make-believe. Your husband, for instance, is ambitious and hard, but his make-believe is to be completely trusting. So, thanks to their short-sightedness, we run naked through the world, with our senses, and freedom of movement, and pleasures of the body. But if one woman betrays us, and for five minutes gives a man clear sight, they all start being, not *really* indignant and revengeful, but *playing* at indignation and revenge. And they get too carried away by their game to stop short of a scandal.

LUCILE: And so?

PAOLA: So I speak to you without any apology, because I'm speaking for every woman. I have to tell you that we've been watching you very closely for some time. And there are some of us who are not going to tolerate the way you're behaving.

LUCILE: Explain yourself.

PAOLA: The explanations are over. Now I'll prescribe for you. When you see a friend going off to visit her lover, you will give her your hand, and when she's returning, you'll smile at her; you'll talk and laugh with the deceived, indulgent husband. You will make quite sure that what you do won't lead a man into making believe he sees things as they are, and perhaps committing a crime.

LUCILE: Or else?

PAOLA: Or else, nothing. Or else an illustration of the divine law: scandal rebounds on to whoever provokes it. Who draws the sword shall perish by the sword. Who lifts the veil must draw aside the shroud. You can choose your own text. And now, my dear, I can smile at you. It's a long-term smile, you don't have to return it before tomorrow. But you will speak to my husband today, indeed now, because here he is.

LUCILE: I'm quite ready to.

Armand has come back with a wrap over his arm.

PAOLA: Armand, Madame Blanchard would like to speak to you.

ARMAND: Unnecessary. I know what Madame Blanchard has to say.

PAOLA: Surely not, darling: surely not.

ARMAND: I'm listening.

LUCILE: You must forgive me for not answering you. It was wrong of me. Silence isn't the way to speak to a man like yourself. Though it may have helped you. Up to now I have given you the silence of a child; now you shall have the words of a woman. I owe this change to your wife. Thank her, as I do. She has made me see that you're not the conceited, hypocritical husband I thought you, but a good and suffering man. If I'm to believe her, a woman is going to speak the truth to a man for the first time. Apparently this means I am going to betray every woman in the world, but this I don't believe, because it's the only way I can keep faith with myself. I mean by repeating to you, like a traitor, what she has been confiding to me; by telling you, like a spy, her naked secrets. Your wife is a monster. She has been unfaithful to you twenty times over, a hundred times. I'm not talking about the men she calls her lovers, Bertrand or Jean-Paul or Guy. She continually deceives you with every living human being. You're not a man at all to her: you're simply the lay-figure of a man who is there to keep her secure in the love of men when the man she loves is tired of her. Leave her. It's better to have twenty-four hours of truth a day than twenty-four hours of lies. Twenty-four hours of honour instead of twenty-four hours of shame. Leave her; it will give you the chance to rediscover all the things you've been missing for some time, the good opinion of the world, of the natural world, of animals and trees; and, more important still, you will have your own good opinion, and you will have mine.

ARMAND: Very well. It shall be done . . . Good-bye, Paola.

PAOLA: Where are you going?

ARMAND: It's done. It's the easiest thing in the world to change one's life. Thank you, madam.

PAOLA: Armand!

ARMAND: How easy it is! Why, everything that belongs to a married couple knows, of its own accord, how it ought to be divided when the couple separate. I can see just how the household is arranging itself: what things go to you, what animals and which of the servants will want to come with me. How unnecessary lawyers really are.

PAOLA: My dearest, what are you doing?

ARMAND: Oh, all you who are tortured by the knowledge that your wife has a lover, imagine she's not your wife any longer, nor will be your wife any longer, and happiness will come back to you.

PAOLA: Armand!

ARMAND: Here's your wrap, Paola. Put it on. You're stark naked.

He goes.

LUCILE: I'm thirsty!

PAOLA: Your thirst can be quenched with water. You're very lucky.

LUCILE: You should be satisfied now; I've spoken to him.

She drinks from a glass into which Paola has dropped a powder, and makes to go.

PAOLA: Are you going? Just one moment.

LUCILE: Don't touch me.

PAOLA: Oh yes, I will. When I was a little girl, instead of collecting stamps I had a trick of touching the lips of people I admired or despised. Now I shall add to my collection and touch yours. Why, what's the matter? They're cold.

LUCILE: Let me go.

PAOLA: No. A peculiarity of mine is to measure both the people I love and the people I hate by the same yard-stick. They all rouse the same desire in me, to touch them, or better still to hold them. So I hold you. I will let you go when I think fit. A woman with something in her grasp has fingers more tenacious than the jaws of a bulldog.

LUCILE: Whether you let me go or not, I don't belong to your regiment of women.

PAOLA: You don't belong! You will see what happens to a woman who leaves it.

Lucile faints. Joseph and other onlookers run to her.

JOSEPH: What is it?

PAOLA: Nothing. Only Madame Blanchard helping herself to ten minutes or so of oblivion. Send all these people away, and fetch Barbette the blood-letter, from across the road.

Joseph and the Customers retire.

Well, there you are. There you are, fast asleep. But this sleep is going to carry you to a shore you never imagined you would visit . . . How beautiful you look, my little enemy, beautiful and precise, as perfectly cut and finished as a key. What am I going to unlock with you, I wonder? Scandal? Disaster? We shall soon see. The moulding and notching of this beautiful key makes it all very promising; it will be a considerable scandal, an unprecedented disaster. I have here the golden key of Pandora's box. And it's just as you wanted it, Lucile; you wanted to unlock hatred and let it out.

Barbette enters hurriedly.

BARBETTE: The poor woman! What can I do?

PAOLA: You can help me to take a revenge. On her. A better work of revenge than you ever did for me before. I'll pay you double.

BARBETTE: A thorn in a facial nerve, shall it be? Or that drug to make her come out in sores?

PAOLA: Certainly not. She's one of those high-minded souls who become more beautiful with adversity. Is your house on the Brignoles road still empty?

BARBETTE: Yes, it is. There are clean sheets on the bed.

PAOLA: You will have to soil them. How quiet, clear, and innocent her sleep is. And what a scent floats out of her. It's not like that with you and me, Barbette; what escapes from us, when the sun has gone down, is the bitterness of the world, which the trees drink in to their cost. What a beautiful night it would be for men if there was nothing on earth except the trees and this woman.

BARBETTE: What has she done to you?

PAOLA: She denounced us.

BARBETTE: Both of us?

PAOLA: All of us. From Cleopatra to Barbette, along with the Queen of Sheba and the town clerk's wife.

BARBETTE: To the police?

PAOLA: To a man. She has told a man that women aren't all angels.

BARBETTE: Shall I cut off her eyelashes? Shall I make her grow a moustache?

PAOLA: You can take her in my carriage. Then lay her on the bed. Undo her bodice, loosen her stockings, and let down her hair. Lying dishevelled is a splendour she never knew with her law-giving husband, her god the judge. So give it to her. Flowers on the table, but the vase knocked over. Sandalwood at the bedside, but crushed under foot. The taste of honey in her mouth, but running on to her chin. Charm her senses before she feels her loathing for the bed.

BARBETTE: It would be dangerous to send a client in to her.

PAOLA: Nothing need happen; it's enough if she thinks it happened.

BARBETTE: Who shall I say it was? An old man would be amusing. An old tramp.

PAOLA: Not with her. No, it should be the most handsome man possible, the best bred and the most subtly corrupting.

BARBETTE: Count Marcellus?

PAOLA: Count Marcellus. Here is his handkerchief. I took it from him as I went past. Make sure that she has it in her hand. Now I leave her to you. But arrange things so that when she first wakes, before she sees herself, she feels she has had a heavenly dream. Take this handkerchief, then. That's right, keep good hold of it. It is woven with Ariadne's thread and leads irrevocably to disaster.

Curtain

170

ACT TWO

Marcellus's house or apartment. Paola. Marcellus.

MARCELLUS: Well, what's brought you here, so early in the morning? It isn't last year now.

PAOLA: This is your wedding morning.

MARCELLUS: Are you the bride?

PAOLA: No, I'm not here to be compensated. I mean a true marriage, Marcellus. One that you'll thank me for.

MARCELLUS: I doubt that. What true marriages do you know in this world?

PAOLA: I know a very interesting one. Vice with virtue.

MARCELLUS: Vice! You're talking like Mr Justice Blanchard, and he talks like an old maid, and she talks like God. You can't expect a man to be Vice at eight o'clock in the morning. At that hour of the day Vice is essentially feminine.

PAOLA: I know you have a theory that men wake up each morning thoroughly newly born. Whatever they are at any other time, in the morning they're spotless children of the new day.

MARCELLUS: Yes, you might say that. Which is why you used to disturb me so last year, always insisting we should meet at dawn. You should know that when a man wakes he is always in the arms of his true wife, whoever is lying beside him. And it takes a certain time to forget her. You definitely used to arrive too early.

PAOLA: If you have a true wife it's cowardice, and the same is true of any man. He trusts himself to the arms of cowardice when he goes to sleep. A sleeping man is a sad sight for a woman who loves him. It's a sleep that rejects her altogether. You sleep without your desire, Marcellus, without your needs, and without your strength, like Lionel Blanchard sleeping without his decorations.

MARCELLUS: Without his decorations? I doubt that. But at any rate he sleeps with Madame Blanchard, which is what I find hard to forgive him; and I mean to make him pay for it.

PAOLA: And if he isn't the only one, would he be so hard to forgive?

MARCELLUS: Your cynicism is losing quality, Paola. Cynicism, like modesty, should come straight from the heart.

PAOLA: Do you think I am jealous of Madame Blanchard?

MARCELLUS: I think you're jealous of innocent women in general. If you didn't know that, I'm telling you now. And I suggest you should be on your guard against it. You become very provincial whenever you're with them. You follow them about, and study them, as though purity were a secret which could be learnt. You look as though you were trying to catch up with the latest fashion; like someone anxious to copy a hat, or remember the details of a dress: to find the secret. The secret you will never know: how to caress a man without seeing him, how to see him without defining him: the secret of Lucrece, and of Madame Blanchard.

PAOLA: Choose better examples. I'm not reliable on the subject of Lucrece. But since nine o'clock last night Madame Blanchard doesn't come into your category at all.

MARCELLUS: That's a lie!

PAOLA: What vehemence!

MARCELLUS: Only what it would be if you told me you were an inexperienced girl again.

PAOLA: Even so, it's the truth. Madame Blanchard has fallen, as they say, prey to a seducer. It was at Barbette's house; Barbette saw everything.

MARCELLUS: Barbette is lying.

PAOLA: Men are so unsubtle. As soon as they see a woman they want, they think they can behave like a husband and demand proofs of fidelity. Well, here they are. Here is a comb that Barbette picked up. And here is the man's handkerchief.

MARCELLUS: Tell me his name!

PAOLA: This is where you shout "Hell and damnation!" I know it's on the tip of your tongue.

MARCELLUS: Tell me his name!

PAOLA: I hesitate to do that. You wouldn't believe me.

MARCELLUS: I kept waking up in the night, and found myself really trembling with joy. There I lay, going through in my mind the time-table of Madame Blanchard's day, thinking of the best way to trap her. It was the first time in my life a conquest was also going to help me to have my revenge.

PAOLA: Are you sure it was only for revenge? From what I saw yesterday, it looked as if revenge was handing the affair over to something softer hearted. And I noticed that though she pretends to see some unpleasant crawling creature on anyone not strictly chaste, she could see no such thing on you. But I can.

MARCELLUS: Ever since that woman came here I've thought of nobody else. You know that. It was a great favour the law-courts did me when they sent her here. Before that I'd only seen virtue in women whose virtue was easy; I'd made the most of glimpses of truth among the lies, touches of grace in the graceless, and so forth. The man who forestalled me with her can have done it only by force.

PAOLA: Quite so. By a pure and simple outrage.

MARCELLUS: What's the name of this brute? He'll answer to me for it!

PAOLA: Don't hurt him too much. It's you, it's yourself.

MARCELLUS: That is a poor joke.

PAOLA: I'm not joking. Your face is the only one that Madame Blanchard can see just now. Her lips are tightly shut on your name and no other. A shadow, with the weight of your bones and flesh, has glided in between her and everything surrounding her, between her and her husband, and her old Marseilles dinner service, and her poodle, and God.

MARCELLUS: What exactly are you trying to tell me! Explain what you mean! Has she noticed me?

PAOLA: She loathes you. You're the first person she's ever hated, so it has all the energy of the first hatred the world ever knew. She has undoubtedly noticed you; she has marked you down for the rest of time.

MARCELLUS: Did Joseph tell her about my speech?

PAOLA (*slowly*): Yesterday, at about seven o'clock, she fainted.

She came to herself during the night, lying on Barbette's bed, half undressed and generally distraught. She learned from her hostess that a man had brought her there, had shut himself in with her, and the man was you.

MARCELLUS: Who invented this ridiculous story?

PAOLA: Revenge. Female vengeance.

MARCELLUS: How can she believe it?

PAOLA: Barbette has faked up a hundred women to seem like virgins in her time. For once, she had to do the opposite, and you can be sure she did it splendidly. And anyway, the victim was clutching your handkerchief. That's the tradition. I know my classics. And now thank me.

MARCELLUS: For giving away to my shadow what I was going to get for myself?

PAOLA: Don't exaggerate. Your charms are on the decline. I took so much trouble to let you into my cousin Celestina's house on Saturday, and you couldn't even succeed with her.

MARCELLUS: Celestina doesn't prove anything. Celestina was perfectly willing, but she had some milk on the fire.

PAOLA: Well, it's now we shall see how much your reputation is worth, Marcellus my dear. Madame Blanchard is yours, if you want her. I know what she's like. She is purity itself, and purity, like sanctity, is imagination overflowing. Can't you see what power over her I've already given you?

MARCELLUS: Go on with your story. Where is she now? You were there at Barbette's house. You followed her there and spied on her. I know what you are: you like to see the evil you're doing.

PAOLA: And the good, too, if you remember?

MARCELLUS: What did she say?

PAOLA: She didn't say anything. She listened to everything Barbette told her, and said nothing. Barbette maintains that her clothes and her hair tidied themselves of their own accord. She didn't ever want to touch herself again, though she has since discovered that won't be easy. One of her knees soon brushed against the other. The contact was awful to her! And there are mirrors in her room at home. By now her eyes will have met their own reflection.

MARCELLUS: So she has gone home?

PAOLA: She went off aimlessly into the dark, like a sleep-walker, holding herself straight and stiff. She neither touched the chapel wall she was passing, nor the dog which jumped up to her. She leaned over the bridge without touching the parapet: no expression in her eyes as she looked down at the river. A white owl wheeled over her head. She looked up at the owl; but nothing more came of it. And then suddenly she weakened; she dared to touch a tree, a young, proud-looking tree, with a round, smooth trunk, something between an aspen and a lime.

MARCELLUS: The limes are in flower. You could have known it by the scent.

PAOLA: Then it wasn't a lime. Any scent would have made her fly for her life. The tree was breathing and whispering, with a tenderness unusual in a tree. So she left it and went on. She must have remembered that her husband was away, and now she had reached home again. She stared up at the house for a long time, and then she went in. I'll swear to you she didn't touch the door. Midnight struck, just as she crossed the threshold. She stopped dead. It was already the day after her crime. The light was on in her room for a long while afterwards. Poor woman! All the perfumes of Arabia wouldn't sweeten a stain which in fact doesn't exist. So now, Marcellus, to work. Her husband won't be back today. Now it's your turn.

MARCELLUS: I'll go there. I don't think much of my chances. But I'm in the mood to content myself with a scandal.

PAOLA: Your chances couldn't be better. Understand that. She doesn't belong to her husband any more. She may refuse. But these women who don't hold with love, are all the more likely to believe in possession – she belongs to you. All you have to do is to take her back. You don't have to compete with the judge any more: only with your own ghost. So as long as you're not inferior to that, all is well.

MARCELLUS: Which is her room?

PAOLA: On the first floor: the door at the far end as you go through her husband's office. You're in riding breeches; that's wonderful. There's nothing so impressive as a good horseman climbing the stairs.

A bell rings. Pause. Enter a Manservant.

MARCELLUS: What is it?

SERVANT: There's a lady to see you, sir.

MARCELLUS: Who?

SERVANT: She wouldn't give a name, sir; I don't know her.

MARCELLUS: Is she wearing a veil?

SERVANT: No, sir; no veil.

PAOLA: Is she a nervous lady?

SERVANT: No, madam; the calmest that ever came here.

PAOLA: With clear grey eyes?

SERVANT: Yes, madam.

MARCELLUS: Ask her to come up.

Exit Manservant.

PAOLA: We've been forestalled, Marcellus. I'll go into your room.

MARCELLUS: That's no good to you. You won't be able to overhear anything at all from there.

PAOLA: It's been a tiring night. For the first time, you can let me use your room to sleep in. Here comes the unicorn. You'd better make sure, when she leaves, she's a less legendary animal.

She goes. Enter Lucile.

LUCILE: Are you Count Marcellus?

MARCELLUS: I am.

LUCILE: And since last night isn't it unbearable to be Count Marcellus?

MARCELLUS: It is. But the fact remains.

LUCILE: Wouldn't you give your life to be the Count Marcellus you were yesterday?

MARCELLUS: I gave more than that last night to be what I am today.

LUCILE: To have to face me like this?

MARCELLUS: To have to face you, above all people.

LUCILE: Did you look at yourself in the mirror this morning?

MARCELLUS: I can't stop looking at myself. I look so young and handsome and happy. Did you?

LUCILE: I looked only once. But I saw what I am, and what I have to do. Most clearly.

MARCELLUS: What I saw was someone who had taken his revenge, not on a hypocritical judge, but on my own too casual way of living. It was weighing me down with shoddy vulgarity. But one day I caught sight of something transcendent and inaccessible. I wanted it, no matter how. I got it. If you've come here, expecting to find me shattered with remorse, you'll be disappointed.

LUCILE: I'm not disappointed. I prayed for you to be as you are.

MARCELLUS: I don't know whether the woman you saw in the mirror told you to let justice and hatred loose on my tracks. But from now on I've got one aim in life, and one only. To stay as I am today. Never to touch any other form of nourishment. To go over and over in my mind an hour which no other man in the world has had. And to nourish my spirit, and my language, and my senses, with that memory, until the day I can surprise you a second time, and have the same pleasure again.

LUCILE: I see I was right to come here.

MARCELLUS: But you're not here at all! Don't you believe it for a moment! You're not the woman who's looking at me and talking like this. You are what you were last night: a body unconscious, but willing, with eyes which are seeing nothing but are wide open: a whispering voice, without a word being said. Why are you here? No more pretending! Last night saw the end of the frozen automaton you used to be.

LUCILE: I came to see you.

MARCELLUS: And you do see me. You saw me yesterday, in your sleep. You recognized then the one who had been promised to you, though you kept your need of him even hidden from yourself. But when he was going away you clung to him.

LUCILE: I'm not clinging to you now.

MARCELLUS: But you will again. If not today, then tomorrow. You've understood that I was never in love before, but I am now.

LUCILE: Did you make these protestations to me when I couldn't hear them?

MARCELLUS: Yes, but you did hear them. And answered me with your body, clear promises, without the least shadow of doubt.

LUCILE: Have you a wife and children?

MARCELLUS: I have a wife. You, by one day.

LUCILE: She is my concern. I've heard people speak of a Countess Marcellus.

MARCELLUS: My mother. Until yesterday she had no cause to be proud of me.

LUCILE: What is she like?

MARCELLUS: On any ceremonial occasion, really beautiful. Particularly at marriages and funerals. A bit too dignified. A trifle opinionated.

LUCILE: Then she will forgive me what I am going to ask you. She will certainly understand . . .

MARCELLUS: You can ask me what you like, without worrying about anyone else.

LUCILE: I know. I have the right, and I mean to take it. But you don't seem to guess what I'm going to ask you.

MARCELLUS: Not yet. Looking at you makes it difficult to concentrate.

LUCILE: And yet it's so obvious. And I haven't any choice. And I don't hesitate to ask you. I know you to be a liar and a trickster, without either generosity or goodness of soul. But I think you've got courage. If I'm wrong, correct me . . . Don't come any nearer.

MARCELLUS: I didn't move. Even at this distance it's so good to see my dear, blind wife with her eyes open at last.

LUCILE: There's honour, I suppose, even in lechery?

MARCELLUS: And to hear my dear, dumb wife speaking.

LUCILE: Then listen to her. For me, there has never been any name but one for the union of a man with a woman. I have been your wife. I am not one of those who, in my position, would agree to say nothing and forget. An atrocious trick has united me with you. It's impossible for me to be united to anyone else. I don't think it's possible to loathe anyone more than I loathe you. If I had to use your Christian name I should vomit blood. If I touched you I should have to cry out. But I can't see how it is possible to ignore the truth as it is in the sight of God: because it was God you compelled to be my witness last night. You have taken me, and poisoned everything, even the things I love. Neither despair nor reason can help me. Your crime has left me nothing to do except give up the only respect I still have any right to, my own self-respect. There's no other way to make myself clean again, and so I have to accept it. I am bound to you; any other tie is broken. My happiness has gone, my beloved husband has been taken away; nothing is left to me except misery and a loathsome husband.

MARCELLUS: Husband! That word's enough to glorify any adjective you give it! Thank you.

LUCILE: Keep your thanks. I don't mean to follow this path like a helpless lamb. I had a different husband yesterday, and I want to find him again. He comes home at dawn tomorrow, and I mean to find him as soon as he returns. I mean his wife to receive him in total loyalty. Without reservation. To-morrow morning he will knock at the door, but it must be still possible for him to be her husband.

MARCELLUS: I defy him to be, and I defy you to be his wife. You've been telling me yourself, since yesterday you're nobody's wife but mine.

LUCILE: I could be a widow.

MARCELLUS: My widow?

LUCILE: I know it would be easy to kill myself. But that's something I don't accept. I've done nothing to deserve death. I saw that when I went back to my home, where I thought everything would cover me with contempt. But everything thought well of me, and had compassion. Even my bed, my marriage-bed, welcomed me as naturally as the bed I slept in when I was little. Not one hour of the night, or of the dawn when it came, made me feel an outcast. If a single stone had told me to kill myself, I should have done so. But the stones told me to live. One growl from a dog would have destroyed me. But the dogs licked my face. But they made one condition: that your wickedness shouldn't leave any mark on me. I would have to transform it into a kind of collision with another period of time, and think of you as belonging to a past already vanished away. You must kill yourself; and then I may be able to speak of you without disgust. Give me your answer.

MARCELLUS: Let me first congratulate myself. I've reached the most beautiful moment of my career: receiving a visit from death, like the engravings of death calling Don Juan to account for all his crimes.

LUCILE: I'm not interested in your crimes. I cling to your death like a child to its mother. It's the only thing that can lead me back to life.

MARCELLUS: I am your husband, Lucile.

LUCILE: I have a black dress. I will wear it tomorrow. Give me your answer.

MARCELLUS: Why this contempt? You know very well what answer I'm going to give.

LUCILE: No, I'm not entirely sure of it. I've been watching you since I came here. Until last night I thought I knew you. But I see now, this was not true. You're as far away from death as a condemned man is from the guillotine. A pity for you. You will have to make the journey on foot.

MARCELLUS: Willingly, but the journey begins with you.

LUCILE: Let me go!

MARCELLUS: Never again. You're not free of your marriage

yet. You still belong to me. And while that is so, even if only for a few hours more, I have the right to ask everything I want from you.

LUCILLE: Oh, God, he's a coward!

MARCELLUS: You're my wife! You've said so. Don't think I'm content with a wedding night which you weren't even aware of. I know what you are myself, caressing and yielding, loving and giving. But you don't know it yet. I suggest that it's time you did. It's beautiful to see virtue arguing with love.

LUCILE: I hate you!

MARCELLUS: You don't hate me. A woman never confesses the truth with her mouth, or even thinks it in her head; it has to be fetched up out of her guts. Which is what I've done.

LUCILE: You've got to die! You've got to die!

MARCELLUS: All right, I'll die. Do you think I'm afraid to do it? I've found you, and I can vanish. Say the word, and I disappear. Any day or hour you like. I give you my word. But only on condition that I can have you in my arms one more time.

LUCILE: I don't hear you.

MARCELLUS: You do hear me, but I'll say it again. If you'll be my wife, just once again, on my honour, I'll kill myself. I'll kill myself immediately afterwards. Do you hear me this time?

LUCILE: No.

MARCELLUS: Your marriage vows call you. Lie down!

ARMAND (*offstage*): Let her alone, Marcellus.

Enter Armand.

MARCELLUS: What do you want here?

ARMAND: What I couldn't be sure I should find. Something like my honour. But fortune favours me. Don't go, madam. You can leave with me presently.

MARCELLUS: Get out of this house.

ARMAND: No. I'm not suggesting the house is mine. But they tell me that my wife used to come here every morning last year. So I have the right to come here one morning this year. One single morning. And I've come at the time she used to come. You won't see me here again.

MARCELLUS: You're late, as a matter of fact.

ARMAND: I was late to start with, I agree. I had come here because of my wife. I was as late as trusting husbands always are when they've been deceived. A year late, or a month, it's all the same. But I've been here some few minutes – the door was on the latch, and I made my way up – I've heard all that you've been saying; and I get the impression that I'm right on time.

LUCILE: Let us go. I must ask you to take me away.

ARMAND: Do what I tell you. Stay here, while I have my say, and say as little as you did in the café yesterday. Your silence today will give me back what your silence took away then. And more.

MARCELLUS: I order you to leave!

ARMAND: I don't take orders from you, though I understand your feelings. I expect it seems odd to you to see a man in your house. Not at all as it should be. He doesn't sit down and look at your pictures, with a beating heart, cooing like a dove. Intolerable. He knows what he's here for. And that's disturbing. You're afraid, aren't you?

MARCELLUS: You may as well know, you're not much good at taking a strong line.

ARMAND: I know I'm not. I'm no good at anything, either as a husband or a friend. That's the way it is. The station in life that I've been called to isn't very seductive. In fact nothing on earth is very seductive, except a seducer.

MARCELLUS: Thanks, and now go.

ARMAND: It wasn't a compliment. A seducer never seduces anybody. He's the poor wretch that other men make use of, to rid themselves of women who're too silly or wanton or over-demanding. You're the victim, my poor chap. Take Paola, for instance . . .

MARCELLUS: Paola has nothing to do with this argument. Paola is a friend of mine, that's all.

ARMAND: You don't really understand anything, Marcellus!
You treat today as though it were like every other day. But
as soon as I opened my window I could see that today is a day
of reckoning. The sky is clear blue, but an invisible line cuts
sheer across it: you can tell at once it's a judgement sky. You
should have opened your window this morning, and looked
at the line in the sky. It would have encouraged you to make
up your accounts. It would also have prompted you to be
honest, and not to say: "Paola is a friend, and that's all". It's
funny how a betrayed husband can't stop talking about his
wife.

MARCELLUS: It's funny how husbands who think they're betrayed are more crass than those who really are.

ARMAND: I'm intelligent. I'm betrayed all right. Poor Paola.
She's as promiscuous as she can be, but she didn't think of
destroying the evidence. She burnt all the letters, never
accepted a portrait, removed every identifying mark from the
gifts she was given. When you gave her roses, she would even
add one or two from our garden, to disguise where they came
from. But she couldn't confuse my memory. As though
everything my unconscious thought wrote on my memory is
being made visible in the light of unhappiness. You've
arrived at the day of reckoning, Marcellus. No denying that
Paola used to come here. She came twenty times, a hundred
times. She knew this room intimately. She used to light these
lamps, or turn them low; she knew these chairs and this sofa
well. If I called out "Paola!" she would come running in
herself. Shall I?

MARCELLUS: You've gone mad.

ARMAND: Don't worry. I won't call her. I shall never call
Paola again. The scent has led me to you and not to her. You
are the one I have to deal with, but not because of Paola.

MARCELLUS: You mean, because of Madame Blanchard.

ARMAND: Precisely. I am happy, Marcellus. Last night I
believed that I was thinking of Paola. There's no doubt my
dreams and the pattern of my thoughts began with her, with
despair and disgust, but now they were all the time turning

towards someone else. Lying awake, I found myself turning from hatred and jealousy towards happiness. To the knowledge that Madame Blanchard was alive and breathing.

MARCELLUS: Madame Blanchard is alive, certainly; and she belongs to me.

ARMAND: We shall see where she belongs. But first of all we both have to kneel down before her, my dear Marcellus. Thanks to her, our poor town has taken a turn for the better. Aix was sadly lacking in greatness and heroism. Madame Blanchard hasn't only brought grace and simple upright living to Aix; she has changed us all, Marcellus, changed you, the untroubled libertine, and me, the untroubled honest husband, and shone a light which seems to have become very like the light of death. All blood and sun! Your shoddiness, and my ingenuousness, are both made bright with death, dear Marcellus. We've no more time to lose. I came here to challenge you, because of Paola, but I found I'd forgotten Paola before I got to your door, and then I overheard your conversation with Madame Blanchard. So now, if you don't mind, it will be because of Madame Blanchard.

MARCELLUS: Just as you like, you ass; I'm entirely at your service. It can be because of every woman who ever came into this house, if that's what you want.

ARMAND: It all comes to the same thing. Anyway, I explain myself badly; your opinion isn't important. If Madame Blanchard agrees, it shall be because of her.

MARCELLUS: And as you well know, since you were spying on us, that's exactly what she wants.

ARMAND: Be quiet . . . I overheard what you said, madam, and I entirely agree. This man broke into your life by a crime, and the only way to rid your life of him may very well be to rid him of his own. With your permission, I'm going to fight him. He has laid my life in ruins, as well. It won't be difficult to see this duel as a judgement of God. What do you say? Are you willing to accept me?

LUCILE: *He* won't be willing. He's a coward.

MARCELLUS: You can send your seconds to me. I shall be at home all the evening.

ARMAND: We can't wait until this evening. Madame Blanchard has suffered too long already. Our seconds are waiting for us in St Mary's fields, with the pistols: I took leave to prepare them, all four of them, yours and mine. None of them turned a hair. They all knew about your affair with Paola. Yours are young Montbaran and your cousin.

MARCELLUS: All right. We'll get little Montbaran to step out the thirty paces. He's got the shortest legs.

ARMAND: There, you see, madam, he isn't a coward. He's vain; vain in a minor sort of way; his blood circulates without a heart. He knows my skill with a pistol, and he's a poor shot himself. He has a very estimable mother. He has a governess who loves him, and dogs that worship him. But he isn't a coward. Are you willing to accept me?

LUCILE (*with a nod*): Yes.

MARCELLUS: Downstairs we go, then, you gallant defender! One thing I'll tell you to put you in good form: the favours of Paola at her most lively are nothing compared with Madame Blanchard's when she's unconscious!

ARMAND: You're taking leave of her now. Is that all you have to say to her?

MARCELLUS: That's all. If she hadn't accepted you, I should probably have told her something else, something which might have been worth at least another kiss to me, and the most grateful kiss of them all. But she'll never hear it now, whether I live or die. Neither will you.

ARMAND: Wait until we have gone, madam, and then go home. You will get news there whether we've lost or won.

LUCILE: Come back again.

ARMAND: Good-bye, madam. Thank you. For today as well as for yesterday.

Exeunt Armand and Marcellus. Enter Paola.

PAOLA: A hard moment for you, Lucile, but here is a friend.

LUCILE: I might have known you wouldn't be far away.

PAOLA: A friend, I promise you. That's not blasphemy. To every new world a new language. And a friend doesn't seem to you now someone to gossip with about clothes and running a house; it means someone to be beside you in this new life of yours, being a woman in a world of men, an accomplice, a twin spirit, a go-between; and all these things I can be.

LUCILE: I knew it! This terrible nightmare is your doing!

PAOLA: What terrible nightmare? The day was bound to come when you would have to give up performing your unconvincing dance of virginity. Love has taken you unaware, while you were asleep, as it probably took Eve unaware in the garden. What a happy thing it would be for us if it were always like that, a great economy of feeling and effort.

LUCILE: Why did you drug me, Paola? Why were you so cowardly?

PAOLA: Paola! At last you've called me by my christian name! The barriers are down!

LUCILE: Be quiet. You are waiting for a man's death, and you are talking.

PAOLA: It's quite proper. People usually talk while they're sitting up with the dead. Look how sisters-in-law who don't like each other quite shamelessly start quarrelling under their breath while they watch by the dying bedside. That's why people in our families die, that the real causes of argument can be brought out into the light of death.

LUCILE: And of hatred, too: don't you think?

PAOLA: Hatred doesn't cure anything, Lucile. You'll come to take a serener, wiser view of this accident presently. And that's just why I came to help you. To you it seems a monstrous wrong, but possible to remedy. Both of those ideas are false. There's no remedy for what happened to you, but it doesn't matter. Love leaves no trace, Lucile. When a woman gets tired of something, it simply isn't there. I sometimes pass men in the street who convey nothing at all to me, who don't touch my imagination, or have any masculine appeal for me whatsoever. You can be sure they were lovers of mine in the past.

LUCILE: Someone rang! Someone is here! They must be back!

PAOLA: No, not they. I do wish you would learn t⹁ know them. They take themselves too seriously to hurry matters. First of all they have to give a dignified bow to the seconds. And at least one of them has to take off his cravat, a most important matter for a man, and the doctor drops his spectacles in the long grass and has to look for them. Even the carriage horses which took them there have a particular slow pace which is called the duelling trot.

LUCILE: You're talking so much, Paola. You're not at ease in your mind. And when someone like you, who has all the graces and all the vices, launches such an attack on someone like me, the only reason there can be for it is that you're afraid.

PAOLA: Afraid of you?

LUCILE: No, not of me – yourself. For I know you despise yourself at this moment. Face to face with me, you feel small and ashamed that you can't stop being ironical and spiteful when I'm suffering.

PAOLA: You're in a melodrama, and I'm in real life. There's a fundamental discord there.

LUCILE: Don't try to drag me over to your side of life. Here, at my own level of unhappiness, I can count on all the resources of God, from miracles to death. I stand beside those who found help for their suffering in turning away from this corrupt world, and confiding instead in a world where everything is possible. You won't bring me down to yours.

PAOLA: It's rather presumptuous, don't you think, over an accident as slight and venial as yours is, to call out for help to the saints and martyrs?

LUCILE: One calls on whoever will reply. When I called, all those women answered who know that what has been done can be redeemed. Those who were stripped naked in front of the crowd, and yet made a cloak out of their nakedness and crossed the town by the main streets. Those whose nails were torn off, and the blood on their fingers became heavenly nails, and they went on with their work. Or those who were stretched over a fire, and the bars of the grid-iron branded heavenly music on their bodies, and they rose up singing. They have all reassured me that presently I shall return calm and unaltered. I shall lie on my bed tonight as untouched as I was before. The price of this is Marcellus's death, but since it was God who faced me with this dilemma, it is God who is giving him his death, and not I. And now God is giving you your answer. Armand has come back.

Enter the Manservant.

SERVANT: Mr Justice Blanchard is downstairs, madam.

LUCILE: Heavens!

PAOLA: What does he want?

SERVANT: He heard that Madame Blanchard was here. He's waiting for her.

PAOLA: A pause in the high drama, while we indulge in a scene of domestic comedy.

LUCILE: Did you send for him?

PAOLA: No, but I expected him, and it's your own fault he has come. Yesterday, in the café, you inconsiderately betrayed all the women in the world, and roused all the men to a hue-and-cry. Today, from one side of the world to the other, the men are going to arrive too soon, leave too late, guess correctly, intercept the incriminating letter and make themselves thoroughly insupportable. God has been pipped at the post by your husband. You can't blame anybody except yourself. What will you decide to do?

LUCILE: I don't want him to see me! I don't want anyone to see me, until Armand has come back.

PAOLA: It doesn't matter so much if your husband sees you. He's not going to notice that your lips are a little riper, and your eyes the faintest degree larger; no husband would. What matters is that you will see him, and see him with the eyes of a woman who has been unfaithful to him for the first time; after years of being blind to him you are going to see him as he really is. That's what is terrifying you, and I can understand it. And that's my revenge, Lucile. You will

see him in his total reality. Yesterday he was simple, generous, and good. What is he going to be when he comes in
through that door? You will never have seen a man you
knew less about.

LUCILE: Very well. Let him come in. He can know everything.

PAOLA: Don't be idiotic, and do make some effort to understand me. However much I may hate a woman, she still ranks
higher with me than any man does, and you and I are going
to be great friends yet. By wrestling naked together, as we
have since yesterday, we've gained an understanding which
has certain duties. Take this staircase here, it leads down to
the street. Your husband knows nothing. I shall tell him that
you came here out of friendship for me, to help me through
an ordeal, and that you've already left again. I'll keep him
here long enough to give you time to get quietly home.

LUCILE: Good-bye.

PAOLA: Au revoir, Lucile, until this evening when we shall sit
like sisters eating our ices under the lime trees, as though
nothing had happened.

LUCILE: Never!

PAOLA: Oh yes, Lucile.

LUCILE: I can never be one of your kind. Your devilish tricks
are no use. Hissing like a snake isn't going to do you any
good.

Exit Lucile.

PAOLA (*slowly, taking pleasure in hissing the words*): Oh yes,
Lucile, it is, yes, it is!

Curtain

ACT THREE

Mr Justice Blanchard's house. His private office, which leads to his room, and Lucile's. Busts of Cujas and Lycurgus. Lionel Blanchard. The Clerk of the Court.

BLANCHARD (*at his table*): Give me the interrogations in the Thomasse case. Cavaillon tells me that it's going to be heard this afternoon.

CLERK: I'll fetch them for you, sir.

BLANCHARD: Did no one tell you I was back?

CLERK: I have just seen Madame Blanchard on the stairs. She went past without speaking to me.

BLANCHARD: You must have made a mistake. Madame Blanchard isn't here.

CLERK: Then you'll find her double in her room, sir. I saw her go in.

Exit the Clerk. Blanchard hesitates, rises, and knocks at Lucile's door.

BLANCHARD: Are you there, Lucile? . . . Lucile! Lucile!

He hears the Clerk coming back, and returns to his table.

CLERK: Thomasse is still protesting that he's not guilty, sir, and goes on stuffing himself with olives.

BLANCHARD: So the Investigation can't get him to confess, before the trial begins, that he killed his wife?

CLERK: Not yet. They're going to stop the supply of olives at noon today.

BLANCHARD: The Investigation has already, successively and quite uselessly, in the order in which he most enjoys them, deprived him of artichokes, tomatoes, and pimentoes. As a form of torture, it seems less effective than the thumbscrew. The statement of the first witnesses?

CLERK: I'll fetch them for you, sir.

He goes out. Blanchard rises and knocks at Lucile's door.

BLANCHARD: Lucile! It is I, Lionel! I was called back home, by express message. Are you there? You are there! I can hear you. Open the door, dearest . . . Why is this? You've locked yourself in! Please, my dear, open the door. Even if you're busy writing a letter to slip into my hand before the trial, one of your sweet letters wishing me good luck in my speech to the Court.

As the Clerk returns, Blanchard goes back to his desk and signs the papers which the Clerk brings him.

CLERK: All the same, sir, this depriving him of things: it was successful in the Tourmaire case. Tourmaire had killed his father, you may remember, and wouldn't confess it. Depriving him of cabbage salad got the most hair-raising details out of him. He heated hairpins in the fire, you remember, and when they were white hot . . .

BLANCHARD: What was the exact date he was committed?

CLERK: I'll fetch it for you, sir.

BLANCHARD: When I ring for you. I have some work to do.

The Clerk goes out. A servant has brought in some flowers which he puts down on a table. Blanchard goes back to Lucile's door.

Lucile, are you ill? Do answer me. Say something! If you don't open the door, Lucile, I shall force it!

The door opens. Enter Lucile.

Well, at last, Lucile!

LUCILE: Lionel, why have you come back so soon?

BLANCHARD: So soon!

LUCILE: Why did you knock? Why did you make me open the door?

BLANCHARD: I thought you must have fainted, Lucile dear. I didn't know what to think.

LUCILE: You didn't know what to think! What do you think now?

BLANCHARD: I breathe again. I see my wife, my adorable wife again, and I've brought her some flowers.

LUCILE: Flowers! Armand wasn't so blind.

BLANCHARD: You mustn't let the duel upset you. Paola warned me about it, and I've sent the mounted police to stop them fighting.

LUCILE: Will they get there in time?

BLANCHARD: They've gone at a gallop. It's worth it if they can save Armand's life. Marcellus is a good shot.

LUCILE: And surely a good target, as well?

BLANCHARD: I hope you weren't displeased that I went to his house to look for you? You'll have to forgive me. When I got back I couldn't stand being in the house without you. What vase shall we have the flowers in? The Meissen?

LUCILE: What was the house like without me?

BLANCHARD: Full of you, just as it is now, even though you weren't there. You're making strawberry jam, aren't you? An incredible scent; I love it. If the Investigation deprives me of it I shall publicly confess to loving you . . . I sat down at this desk, and looked at the pens and the sharpened pencils you had put ready for me, and felt loved and waited for. I took up this new pen, blessed you for remembering it was my favourite kind, and corrected my indictment. By far the most fascinating one of my career: this Thomasse case: he killed his wife. It's a pity that the world's first murder was a man killing a man; it means I can't refer to it in my speech. But my reference to the first woman ever killed by a husband, Sara her name was, is very fine; it ought to make a great impression on the Court, I think. I rehearsed the whole speech in front of the mirror. But you weren't there, as you've always been before, to help me with your opinion. It was no use. My little Lucile hadn't slipped into the robes of Justice, to help me in the pursuit of crime. So I had to go and find you.

LUCILE: And have you found me now?

BLANCHARD: Indeed I have.

LUCILE: And you'll take me in your arms? Will you kiss me?

BLANCHARD: With the tenderest recognition that a husband and magistrate responsible for the Thomasse case has ever felt.

LUCILE: Can you see me quite clearly?

BLANCHARD: Wonderfully.

LUCILE: Let me go.

BLANCHARD: I'm sorry.

LUCILE: Lionel, I've changed since yesterday. Don't you see?

BLANCHARD: Your dress, you mean? Or altered in looks? I don't see any difference.

LUCILE: My hair, my dress, my mouth. Surely you see?

BLANCHARD: Your mouth? What are you talking about? Tell me what to look for.

LUCILE: It's so clear, so obvious. And you can't see.

BLANCHARD: Lucile, you're raving! What has happened to you? What were you doing yesterday?

LUCILE: What were you doing yesterday, Lionel, at eight o'clock?

BLANCHARD: Oh, good heavens, now I understand! You've been feeling jealous! Well, that's very gratifying; and in answer to the counsel for the prosecution, my darling wife, yesterday at eight o'clock, on the twenty-ninth of July, I was dining at Cavaillon with Counsellor Provenchères. At that precise moment he was opening a bottle of Château-Châlon which he gets direct from the Scee family themselves; he's related to them by marriage. It's a "vin de paille", as you probably know, rather like Tokay, the parent vine was brought from Hungary by an abbess, who travelled with it hidden in her sleeve. It's a strong wine, but dry. We drank your health in it.

LUCILE: And you didn't find a scorpion at the bottom of the bottle?

BLANCHARD: Not at all. And the Strasbourg pâté was remarkably free from earwigs and centipedes.

LUCILE: Then you were no clearer-sighted yesterday than you are today. Lionel, listen; don't ask any questions, just do what I tell you. Go away, leave at once! I beg you to. Your carriage is still harnessed. Come back tomorrow at the time you meant to come. Everything will be all right again tomorrow.

BLANCHARD: But what's the matter? You've changed, you say! But I'm the one you are looking at as though I'm not the same person any longer.

LUCILE: You will be tomorrow! Please go.

BLANCHARD: Lucile, my dear, I haven't been able to take you with me up to the present. I've had to do all the accumulation of work which my predecessors so obligingly left to be done. Don't blame me for that; from now on you won't ever have to be parted from me. I've bought a new carriage which I was keeping as a surprise for you. It's got a special chest for carrying cold meals, and a canteen of folding forks and collapsible cups, with our monogram on. I've ordered you a new carriage cape from Grenoble, because the wind is very keen on the moors; and the field glasses you've always wanted, so that you can follow the birds up into the sky, and pick out any ghosts that may be wandering about in the castle ruins as we go past. But there's a point I must make clear to you. The success of a man's career is based, more than anything else, on a woman's even temper and reliability. The foundation of every successful enterprise a man undertakes, the root of every fruitful career, is a woman who doesn't change, in looks, or gesture, or voice. As one of my Roman predecessors so wisely said: *Ab una uxore unus vir. Una* to be understood in the sense of "uniformity", and *unus* in its sense of "uniqueness". A unique man will always be found to have an equable wife; and the same thing applies to men of talent and brilliance, and, as in my own case, Lucile, of justice. I lead a full, rich, and useful life because I don't have to negotiate all the complicated lock-gates of temperament, and uncertainties of the heart. This is the first time that I've looked at you and seen a face I don't quite recognize . . . Has my cravat come loose? What's wrong with it? . . . No! You shall not go back to your room! I forbid you to!

LUCILE: Lionel, please! Let me alone, at least until we've had news of the duel!

BLANCHARD: You've got this duel on the brain. I can promise you there won't be any duel. By the time they've decided which of the seconds shall pace out the distance, and long before the duellists have had time to take off their coats and untie their cravats, my police will have caught up with them. Sit down here beside me.

LUCILE: Then I must ask one question, Lionel.

BLANCHARD: When I've revised my indictment. I'll read it to you. Concentrate; you can be as critical as you like.

LUCILE: Lionel, it's a sort of question like a flash of lightning. If the mind doesn't answer it with the same speed, it can't be asked again. It is over for ever.

BLANCHARD: It isn't exactly a magistrate's *forte* to reply to flashes of lightning.

LUCILE: But suppose, early in my life, I'd had another husband, and was now a widow. You find that out. Would you take me back again? Would you marry me again?

BLANCHARD: Stop all this childish nonsense. If another man had touched my wife, whether the calendar went forwards or backwards, I wouldn't see her again as long as I lived.

LUCILE: Remembering she had been unconscious, Lionel, lifeless and unconscious.

BLANCHARD: The flesh is never unconscious.

LUCILE: The flesh! How can you use that terrible word to me? To say I have flesh!

BLANCHARD: You force me to. There are a thousand different ways of talking of the spirit, but the flesh is the flesh, even when it's yours. If a man had touched my wife, I should never touch her or speak to her again for the rest of my life.

LUCILE: Then, good-bye . . .

BLANCHARD: But what has happened? What are you trying to tell me?

LUCILE: What has happened is that you'll never touch me again. You'll never speak another word to me.

BLANCHARD: A man has dared to lay hands on you?

LUCILE: He has dared to marry me.

BLANCHARD: Stop using that ridiculous word! A man has touched you!

LUCILE: My word is the right word. Why did you come back

so soon, Lionel? Everything good and innocent was rallying to help me. By coming home so soon, you've spoilt it all.

BLANCHARD: It's Marcellus! That's why you went to his house.

LUCILE: He drugged me last night, and carried me to one of his houses. I woke up, and Marcellus had gone.

BLANCHARD: Swear to me, swear that's true.

LUCILE: I didn't even see him. The reason I went to his house this morning . . .

BLANCHARD: Was to give this crime a face and a voice, to give him eyes to see you with!

LUCILE: Was to ask him to kill himself. And almost at the same moment Armand came to challenge him because of Paola. And now I'm waiting.

BLANCHARD: And you've even left it to someone other than me to avenge your honour.

LUCILE: I still keep my honour; it's the only thing that's not destroyed in me.

BLANCHARD: And you dare to call this degrading incident your second marriage!

LUCILE: It's the only way I could purify it. You, too! You, too!

BLANCHARD: You dare to say they were a husband's kisses that he gave you!

LUCILE: Oh, Lionel, do believe me, listen to me.

BLANCHARD: So you insist on calling yourself his wife until he's dead!

LUCILE: There may be only a minute to wait, only two minutes.

BLANCHARD: It won't be many more, whatever happens. (*He takes pistols from a drawer.*)

LUCILE: Lionel, Lionel dear!

Blanchard goes, bumping into the Clerk.

CLERK: M. Blanchard, sir! Sir!

LUCILE: What do you want him for?

CLERK: Madam, the most important exhibit in the Thomasse case has disappeared out of the cupboard! The phial of poison. I put it there yesterday evening.

LUCILE: You'd better hurry and find it. Go and look for it quickly!

The Clerk goes. Enter Armand.

ARMAND: Good-bye, Lucile.

LUCILE: He's dead!

ARMAND: He's dying. I managed to avoid the police. I wanted to see you again before they arrested me.

LUCILE: He's dead!

ARMAND: He was condemned to die. God had stricken him with the malady which he gives to anyone he means to lose: made him slow.

LUCILE: Oh, Armand, it's too late.

ARMAND: I came here at a gallop. But I know your husband's coach has been quicker, and quicker than death, as well.

LUCILE: Yes. He's home.

ARMAND: But Marcellus has gone. The only thing that matters.

LUCILE (*after a pause*): Armand, are you sure of that?

ARMAND: So far as I feel I'm an avenger and not a murderer, yes.

LUCILE: Forgive me, Armand. But I think I have been wrong.

ARMAND: Wrong to be true to yourself?

LUCILE: To have had so much pride. Why should I have told Marcellus I was his wife? To have called it a marriage, instead of quite simply a great misfortune. Why wasn't I content to be the dishonoured wife with a loving, unhappy husband?

ARMAND: You still can be. The husband and the unhappiness are both still there.

LUCILE: That's just what I don't know, Armand. That's what is so frightening. The man I've just seen isn't the husband I thought he was yesterday. I've seen a man I never saw before, someone I never loved.

ARMAND: In a moment of shock a man can't always find the right mask to wear, to face the disaster. The mask of the outraged husband was in easy reach, and he took it. Give him time to put it down and you'll see his real face again.

LUCILE: All my life I won't forget the other. Oh, Armand, it's dreadful to think that if you take a man's wife away from him, he is changed from someone just and good and generous, into an egotistical bully. But that's what I've seen with my own eyes. His wonderful cloak of virtue, which he was so proud of, as I was, too, has fallen suddenly into rags. Everything he says sounds like hypocrisy and wrong-thinking, even though he is using words like honour and justice and the family. He quoted Latin as if he had lifted up a gravestone. Even the scent of the lotion on his chin, which I chose for him, and the cloth his suit is made of, which I also chose, were as alien and hostile to me as he was.

ARMAND (*after a pause*): Why are you telling me these things which you should only tell yourself?

LUCILE: So that you can reassure me. Oh, Armand, tell me what a man is, drive away this nightmare, and I'll believe you.

ARMAND: What a man is? From what I know of myself, all I can say is that he's neither complicated nor unique.

LUCILE: But generous and strong, isn't that so?

ARMAND: Gullible and unreal. He believes, first of all, if he's modest, that the world belongs to him completely. Then, if he's intelligent, he believes that woman belongs to him, and love belongs to him. Then, when his hope in life has given place to the pleasures of living, he groans away the night in silence, and weeps with a dry eye.

LUCILE: Is that everything?

ARMAND: Everything up to yesterday.

LUCILE: Go on. What is he today?

ARMAND: Today he has killed. The harmless one has killed: he is going to prison for murder. He has destroyed his life. He has seen you. He is happy.

LUCILE: Thank you. Lionel can come back. Good-bye.

Enter Paola, followed by Barbette.

PAOLA: What's more, a man is pretentious, if he's one of the simple sort. Weak and feeble, if he's one of the passionate sort. And if he's timid, he gambles with destiny like a madman. And by that, I mean you.

ARMAND: Who have you brought here? Who is this woman?

PAOLA: She is splendid, isn't she? In every way like the destiny I mentioned.

ARMAND: What have you come here for?

PAOLA: To listen to you, amongst other things. It was well worth the trouble. I'm sure that martyrs have never mutually crowned each other with such laurels before. You may think you're defying death, but you're screaming love at each other like a pair of cats. I've come to avenge Marcellus, and it won't be difficult.

ARMAND: Leave Marcellus to his death, where you put him.

PAOLA: Don't quibble. You're the murderers. She killed him. You killed him. You, out of vanity. She, by thinking she was virtuous. You, by the honour of a gentleman. Both of you by chasing after tragedy when you're really deep in farce. But you won't be able to look at each other when I've said what I have to say to her.

ARMAND: Get away from here, or I'll take you away, whether you like it or not.

PAOLA: This woman is a criminal, Armand. If it hadn't been for her, you would still be happy with me, proud of me and rightly so. She understood nothing. She denounced me, without seeing that it was only her denunciation that made me guilty. My life took many different shapes, but not one of them encroached on the others. I wasn't like her; no woman is. She makes a sordid hotch-potch of her body and her sentimentality. Half like a schoolgirl, and half like a witch stirring you, and her husband, and Marcellus, all up together in one cauldron. I loved you yesterday, Armand. You were dearer to me than anyone in the world. If I've had lovers, they were outside our territory, nothing to do with the affection we had for each other. And we're all like that, except Lucile, who hasn't got our gift of forgetting, can't manage our transmigration of soul. I've always loved you completely

and devotedly, with the whole of my being which belonged
to you.

LUCILE: Everything this woman says is untrue. It isn't because
I denounced her to you that she hates me but because I denounced her to herself. She thinks her loose-living is fine-
spirited. She thinks every wicked affair she had was the fine
flower of youth and beauty. And as she got older she would
have become more and more sure of it. Her vicious past
would have seemed correct and dignified. But my voice has
changed all this into a waste of weeds and filth, and execration.

PAOLA: Alas, I have to disappoint you, dear Lucile. I'm handing my past over to you. You belong now to the regiment of
women you refuse to acknowledge. You refuse to acknowledge yourself, now, and that's my revenge. This change in
you, which so delights Armand, this languor, this passion,
this slow, but very successful, alteration from the prudish
magistrate's wife to the frightened woman obsessed by her
predicament, has been brought about by no one but yourself.
Listen to this, Armand. It's true there was a rape last night
on the Brignoles road, but it wasn't Marcellus who was
responsible . . .

LUCILE: Oh, heaven, protect me!

PAOLA: The responsible one is alive. Is there at this moment.
Isn't that so, Barbette?

LUCILE: This woman is Barbette?

PAOLA: She is here to help you. Today even more than yesterday. And her moment has come. Come here, Barbette; and
not as though you were falsehood, when in fact you're truth
itself. She is here with the truth for you, and a truth which is
going to horrify you.

ARMAND: Paola!

PAOLA: It isn't that Marcellus invited some friends to a drunken
orgy, nor that a tramp saw an open window and an unconscious woman, and made the most of it. My revenges aren't
so commonplace, Armand my darling. You're going to fall
on my neck and bless me for this. But Madame Blanchard
will be less relieved. She has a suspicion already that her

dignity and respectability are escaping her: that she isn't Marcellus's widow after all; that this soft, guilty, pulsating body is hers by nature. Because Marcellus hasn't held her in his arms. Barbette is a witness to that. There was no assault last night. This morning she is just as she was yesterday, when she sat eating her strawberry ice, a narrow-minded woman, quite intact, who has never been touched by the hand or lips of anyone, except the honourable husband.

LUCILE: And Marcellus held his tongue. God, pity me!

PAOLA: Your hands are shaking, Lucile. And it isn't just the shame of looking ridiculous. What a disaster it is to lie down a martyr and rise a virgin! You are beginning to feel you have lost the only reason you had for believing in yourself, and you can't bear it.

ARMAND: What is it, Lucile?

LUCILE: Go away! Leave me alone, all of you!

ARMAND: I don't understand.

PAOLA: You will understand tomorrow. Men always understand – tomorrow. There you have the true scandalous story, Lucile. The rape last night was the work of Madame Blanchard herself. A case, you might say, of purity destroying itself. She boasted that she could tell immediately who was sinning, and how and when; but she couldn't recognize her own purity, couldn't tell, after all, that she hadn't been kissed and loved. She believed everything she was told, believed she moaned with joy, believed she held Marcellus back by his arm and his thigh. Sad for her that it's only a shadow.

LUCILE (*to Barbette*): Is this true, what this woman says?

BARBETTE: Yes, madam.

LUCILE: Nobody touched me but you?

BARBETTE: No, madam.

LUCILE: And the mark on my arm?

BARBETTE: I bit you, madam. Quite gently. Your flesh is tender. And the mark above your knee . . .

LUCILE: Did Count Marcellus not come in for a moment, or even see me? How did the handkerchief come to be in my hand?

BARBETTE: Madam put it there.

PAOLA: And brought it back again. And that's the end of that little interlude. And here we are, face to face again, as we were on the café terrace. I can only say again what I was saying then . . .

ARMAND: Come away with me, at once.

PAOLA (*losing control*): I have a mission. I'm going to finish it. (*To Lucile.*) When you see a friend going off to visit her lover, you will give her your hand, and when she's returning, you'll smile at her; you'll talk and laugh with the deceived, indulgent husband. You will make quite sure that what you do won't lead a man into making believe he sees things as they are, and perhaps committing a crime. You can't say now that I'm only pleading my own cause . . . I think I heard your husband's carriage. Good-bye. A dead man is waiting for me, and a policeman is waiting for Armand, and neither of them, as we know, care to be kept waiting.

Blanchard appears, running up the stairs.

LUCILE: Lionel, save me!

BLANCHARD: It's done. You've been made a widow. Your husband, in God's view of time, died under my very eyes. He saw me. He laughed, and called out your name. Blood came out of his mouth, and your name was in it. He vomited the name back to me.

LUCILE: Lionel, listen!

BLANCHARD: He gave your body back as well. But too late.

ARMAND: Listen to her! Will you listen?

BLANCHARD: I know what she has to say. That she knew nothing and felt nothing, that I still have her faithful, uncontaminated soul. But today I'm a husband, and I'm not satisfied with these police court words. What I call a faithful wife is a wife who ceases to exist the moment a strange hand brushes against her. But the hand has touched my wife, taken hold of her, known her, and my wife is here, in health and spirits.

LUCILE: I was unconscious, Lionel.

ARMAND: What are you saying, Lucile?

BLANCHARD: Unconscious! That's even worse! I've been deceived by something deeper than the woman she is in the daytime, gossiping, housekeeping, shopping, the fully conscious woman that everybody knows; I've been deceived by the night-time in her, by the languid, naked sleep, which is what a man is most proud of when he's away from his wife. Leave here, Lucile, leave this house.

LUCILE: There's no need to ask me. I am going.

ARMAND: Lionel, listen to the truth.

LUCILE: Not a word, Armand. Do you hear? Don't say a word.

BLANCHARD: Get out of here, and don't play the victim. It's only too easy to be the victim! Here's a woman who doesn't drink wine, and even sips her quince-water with a certain anxiety, but who can't protect herself from drinking poison. She never loses a handkerchief or a key, she loses herself, and everything that my honour and happiness were made of, from her head to her foot, are swept past me to be squandered on this lecher Marcellus.

ARMAND: Lionel, question this woman here.

BLANCHARD: What a fool I've been, these five years, meekly going on respecting her virtue and innocence, respecting this body, if you please, when it refused every invitation from her husband, only to go and accept a lover. Oh, heavens, instead of all this, all this solemn high-thinking and timidity, what Marcellus-like nights I could have given myself!

LUCILE: There it is. It's over.

ARMAND: Lionel, you're beside yourself! Listen to me! Here is Barbette: it was her house that Lucile was carried off to. I do beg you. Question her.

BLANCHARD: So you were there, were you?

BARBETTE: Yes.

BLANCHARD: I'm listening.

BARBETTE: He undressed her.

ARMAND: What are you talking about, you liar?

BARBETTE: I say what I have to say, isn't that so, madam?

LUCILE: Yes. Thank you, Barbette.

BLANCHARD: And was she unconscious?

BARBETTE: Unconscious. She thanked him, and smiled, but unconsciously.

BLANCHARD: When he was leaving, what did she do?

BARBETTE: With her arms round his waist and his neck, she tried to hold him back, but unconsciously.

BLANCHARD: That's all there is to be said. (*Exit.*)

ARMAND: Lionel, come back! The woman's lying! Lucile, please, you must call him back!

LUCILE: Thank you, Barbette.

ARMAND (*to Paola*): What are you smiling at?

PAOLA: One can smile. There stands Lucile, the woman.

BARBETTE: Well, I took your revenge for you, didn't I, my dear? That's what they're like. He's got his reward. He won't rest quiet again as long as he lives.

PAOLA: Well, Lucile, life is beautiful, is it, life is pure?

LUCILE: It's terrible. Everything is terrible.

PAOLA: Is there still the unbridgeable gulf between what you said was infamous, and what you described as noble?

ARMAND: Take no notice of her, Lucile. For the sake of the future, scorn to listen to her.

PAOLA: The future? There are two possible futures lying in front of Madame Blanchard today. The first is what she calls virtue. She is still obstinate enough, in spite of her downfall, to pick herself up again, and go on like a hypocrite with her career as the magistrate's wife.

ARMAND: And the other future is yours, is it not?

PAOLA: It's mine, it's love: and she would be foolish not to accept it. Anyway the battle is over, and I've won it; and victory is the only virtue there is in the world. Come, Barbette.

LUCILE: Get down on your knees, Paola!

PAOLA: On my knees?

LUCILE: On your knees! To ask a pardon.

PAOLA: To ask pardon of whom?

LUCILE: Of Marcellus. Of our husbands. Of Barbette. Of everyone alive or dead. Of me. Of yourself.

PAOLA: Pardon for what?

LUCILE: For having said that life is without worth or purity.

PAOLA: Well, isn't it? What worth can you see in today, for instance?

LUCILE: Today is horrible. It has mocked at everything, made everything vile.

PAOLA: Then we're in complete agreement, Lucile. It's a defeat for you, and there's no way out of it.

LUCILE: No way out of it? How wrong you are! The way out is here, in my hand. I went for help to a little girl, of my own age and my own name, who swore, when she was ten years old, never to accept evil, swore to prove, even by death if it had to be, that the world was a noble place, and that human beings were pure in heart. Now this world has become empty and terrible to her, and life nothing but corruption; but it doesn't matter, it isn't even true, because she is still going to keep the vow she swore.

BARBETTE: What are you doing? Why do you say this?

PAOLA: What has the little idiot done?

ARMAND: Lucile!

LUCILE: Don't call. There's no cure for this. The Thomasse murder has been good to me. I knew that the poison killed, and without any suffering. And quickly.

BARBETTE: Who made you do it, my poor little one? You weren't in any danger from men, I can tell you that. You were no concern of theirs, you were like an angel.

LUCILE: Armand!

ARMAND: Lucile.

LUCILE: My last wish, Armand! That my husband never knows the truth. Let him believe Barbette. He will live from now on scorning an innocent woman, as she has been scorning him: and admiring the guilty woman who hated life. He will live in a false legend, but what legends are true? Truth is always the poor lamb being sacrificed. What else could I have done, Armand? What else except play the heroine? Heroes are men who glorify a life which they can't bear any longer. And so it has come about with me. Is Paola kneeling?

PAOLA: Yes.

LUCILE: She is still standing, but she said yes. I have won. The world has purity, Paola, beauty, and light. Tell me so yourself. I want to hear you say so. Tell me quickly.

PAOLA: It is true . . . for this moment.

LUCILE: I'm content with that. A moment will do. Thank you. Don't let Paola come near me. Barbette will dress me for burial.

She slips to the ground.

PAOLA: She was called Lucrece, was she not?

Armand leads her away. Lucile dies. The lights darken, and when they grow bright again Barbette is alone with Lucile.

BARBETTE: Dear little creature, my little angel! The others have gone, and now we can talk. There's only God between us, and he has been with you since yesterday. If you had seen how you got up from the bed at midnight, you would know. It was a miracle . . . All the women in the town are talking about it already. You crossed yourself, and your stockings drew themselves on by themselves. Your shoes slipped themselves on to your feet. People have been canonized for less. The flowers I'd put at the bedside, my paper flowers, they breathed out the scent of roses, and when I went to touch them the flowers and the leaves were real. I'm not lying, I promise you; and just let me take this little ring off your finger to keep as a memory of it. You're thinner than you were yesterday, my angel: the ring comes off of its own accord. Mind you, miracles don't make our job any easier: they are bad for business. Purity's not for this world, but every ten years we get a gleam of it. And now all of them, with their intrigues and wicked doings, are going to see themselves standing in the light of it. Standing stock still, looking surprised, as though the photographer was taking them, as though the pure light was drenching their bodies. They will suddenly see it for the holy thing it was, and they'll feel it reproach them . . . It won't last long with them, I know that very well. With women the virtue of one is the virtue of all. Whereas each man lives the lord of his own dunghill, and has to be his own saint, and his own purgatory. Get along with you. We've all understood you; Paola as much as anybody. It's true you were ravished. But not by Marcellus. You could have got over that, fifty women have got over that; you knew yourself you could. But what struck you down was being made aware of man's stupidity, and coarseness, and wickedness, too much all of a sudden. And if you're as tender a creature as you, you die of it. Your brooch is coming undone; that means you're giving it to me, and I'm taking it for a keepsake. There's only this mark of the bite my old mouth gave you that you'll have to explain up there, but don't think twice about it. Show it to them, explain. Tell them it's a kiss to all women from an old bawd in Aix, and you've brought it along as a promise from her that she, and all her sisters of the town, won't give men any rest, neither in the profession nor on the side, neither to the young ones who snigger like fools, nor the old ones with their lecherous grinning, nor the handsome ones, nor the ugly ones, nor the city treasurer, nor the magistrate's clerk who comes as a spy: give no rest to their health, nor their purse, nor their family, nor the marrow of their bones, so as to revenge you, my little angel, and lead them all straight to eternal damnation. Amen.

The curtain falls

NOTE

In performance at the Theatre Royal, Newcastle-upon-Tyne, the following changes were made in the text:

From page 154, line 3 to page 155 line 4 was omitted, and the following was substituted: ARMAND (*turns to Paola and turns back in great fury*): But my wife hasn't deceived me.

On page 157 the last seven lines and on page 158 the first two lines were omitted.

On page 159, lines 15–22 were omitted, and the following was substituted:

EUGÉNIE : Here he is back again.

ARMAND : Yes. I'm back. When men have been talking to a woman they want to see again, they leave their gloves or their stick behind. I left my life on your table, my dear Eugénie, my entire life.

EUGÉNIE : You left your gloves as well. They would have been quite enough.

On page 183, from line 14, "Poor Paolo . . ." to line 22 ". . . light of unhappiness" was omitted.